M000159564

# So THAT'S Why They Do That!

### Men, Women And Their Hormones

"Nobody in recent memory has written the ABCs and XYZs on the connection between sex, relationships and human hormones more satisfyingly than married couple Judith Claire and Frank Wiegers. They demystify famously bumpy terrain (fertility, menopause, testosterone, sexual communication to name a few) by crafting a clear and comprehensive 21st Century roadmap for the genders. If there is one book to solve World Peace by enlightening couples about their bodies, and solving in and out of the bedroom disputes around the globe, it's So THAT'S Why They Do That.  Happy landings, indeed!"

XAQUE GRUBER -- THE HUFFINGTON POST


"Finally, a user's manual for the opposite sex—and to better understanding yourself when it comes to love and lovemaking.  This book distills the wisdom of modern research and practical experience into simple but profound guidelines that will enhance your understanding of the interpersonal dynamics that affect each one of us every day of our lives."

JENNY WADE, RESEARCHER AND AUTHOR OF
TRANSCENDENT SEX: WHEN LOVEMAKING OPENS THE VEIL


"So THAT'S Why They Do That! is an owner's manual for the human body that reveals how to master your hormones throughout your life to increase romance and happiness. It's the perfect "how to" book for men and women. Everyone will get a kick out of reading it."

PAUL J. ZAK, PROFESSOR OF ECONOMICS, MANAGEMENT AND PSYCHOLOGY
AT CLAREMONT GRADUATE UNIVERSITY, AUTHOR OF
THE MORAL MOLECULE: THE SOURCE OF LOVE AND PROSPERITY

# So THAT'S Why They Do That!

## Men, Women And Their Hormones

A TOP GUN LOVE MANUAL BY
### JUDITH CLAIRE & FRANK WIEGERS

TOP GUN LOVE INC. PUBLISHING

# So THAT'S Why They Do That!

## Men, Women And Their Hormones

Published by:

Top Gun Love Inc. Publishing

Santa Monica, CA 90403

www.topgunlove.com

Book design by Marael Sorenson

Cover design by Lee Roesner

Cover photo by Alial

Image source: Alial/Bigstock.com

Back cover photo by Lauren Keskinel

Library of Congress Control Number: 2014936472
ISBN: 978-0-9911622-9-1

## Warning/Disclaimer

# CONTENTS

# INTRODUCTION

My husband, Frank Wiegers, and I believe that creating a loving, fulfilling relationship that includes great sex is one of the most important things you can do in your life. It can also be one of the most challenging. The inspiration behind *So THAT'S Why They Do That! Men, Women And Their Hormones* is to help you achieve that treasured goal.

I've been a personal, career and relationship counselor in Los Angeles for 37 years. During that time, I have had ample opportunity to observe how important it is for people to understand how sex hormones shape the different approaches men and women have to just about everything— from making love, to communicating, to handling stress, to dealing with conflicts. Failure to grasp the underlying biology and psychology of the sexes creates confusion at best and war at worst. Conversely, I've seen how learning what makes the sexes tick vastly improves dating, finding a mate, creating a committed relationship and keeping a marriage healthy and joyful.

Although the book's slant is on love and sex, it also sheds light on, and helps improve other important personal relationships—those with our parents, siblings, children, and friends. In the workplace, it increases our understanding of our seniors, juniors, co-workers and clients. I wish I'd had this information when I was 18.

In dating and couples counseling, I often find my clients blaming their partners for behaviors that are particular to the hormonal makeup of their partner's sex. For example, this conflict brought to you courtesy of Mother Nature: "He never wants to talk about our problems, which leaves me anxious or angry" vs. "She always want to process everything, especially before we go to sleep, which stresses me out." Like the myriad of other problems confronting couples, resolving this one requires understanding and compromise. That in turn begins with realizing that your partner is not flawed, but hormonally programmed to have different needs, abilities and reactions than you. This is equally true for gay couples, because one partner tends to be more masculine and the other more feminine.

My clients range in age from their late teens to well into their 70s, so I get to work with upset men and women in every phase of life. The huge hormonal changes that occur in pregnancy and postpartum, menopause and andropause can create significant physical, emotional and sexual problems that try both the person undergoing the change and their partner.

Relationships can get rocky, just when a team effort is needed the most. It's hard to get in sync and heal anything if you don't really know what's going on.

So THAT'S Why They Do That! is dedicated to demystifying the motives and actions of the opposite sex, as well as your own, in all the stages of your life. The aim is to increase your tolerance and appreciation of the natural differences between men and women, which leads to greater cooperation, love and harmony.

## HOW THIS BOOK IS WRITTEN

So THAT'S Why They Do That! is the first of a series of books my husband and I are writing. Frank is a former fighter pilot turned love, sex and relationship coach. Together we teamed up to form "Top Gun Love" as a means of sharing our two lifetimes worth of experience and knowledge with couples and singles. Using the "Top Gun" analogy, we decided to create our books as manuals, much like the ones Frank used to operate jet aircraft, and to write them from a fighter pilot's perspective.

Our intention is to make all "Top Gun Love" manuals user-friendly to men while still being wholly engaging to women. It's turned out to be a successful strategy. Guys have read So THAT'S Why They Do That! and eagerly shared it with their girlfriends or partners. Women have felt relieved to have something they can show to their men that speaks for them.

The ladies also enthusiastically shared it with girlfriends, family and reading groups.

The first and biggest section in any jet fighter manual is Descriptions and Operations, which gives the nitty-gritty details about every piece of equipment on the plane and how they interact. Pilots have to know this section backwards and forwards before flying. Likewise, there's nothing more basic to male and female behavior than the sex hormones that produce human traits, drives and differences. Learning how these hormones work gives you the understanding and tools to pilot your sex and relationship life through sunny and turbulent skies.

We also use our own versions of other conventions in the fighter pilot's manual.

## CHECKLISTS

A checklist covers almost every phase of flight; it is a list of tasks that have to be performed in a certain order to ensure that the airplane is operated safely. Our "checklists" refer to lists and exercises.

*NOTES, CAUTIONS, WARNINGS:* These are the special annotations flight manuals use to highlight important bits of information and to emphasize the increasingly dangerous consequences of not rigorously following operating procedures and processes. Ours underscore the critical "dos" and "don'ts" of relationships.

Another fun feature is Frank's Air Force anecdotes and personal comments. They are indicated with "quotes" around them. So, although I wrote most of this book while he's been focusing on our next one, *Surefire Sizzling Sex*, it's going to read, by design, as if he wrote it. He also created the graphs and charts and his invaluable insights inform the entire book.

Frank and I hope you begin using *So THAT'S Why They Do That!* immediately as a reference book, turning to it as life happens and thorny gender-related issues arise. We also hope that your new understanding of the fundamental male/female differences shifts the way you interact with the opposite sex, eliminates problems before they happen, and creates sizzling sex and wonderful, lasting relationships.

May you have smooth flights and happy landings!

*Judith*

## IMPORTANT NOTE

As you read these chapters there will be parts where you'll think: "That's not true; I'm not like this." or "My partner isn't like that." You will be right. There are seven billion unique individuals on this planet, all having different DNA, which means we all have varied amounts of male and female sex hormones. We come from different countries, cultures and families and have been exposed to a variety of personal experiences that shape our brains and our behavior. Therefore, you and everyone else are a matchless mix of masculine and feminine characteristics.

What are yours? What are your partner's? Compare the information on sex hormones and see what applies to each of you. It's not only a very enlightening exercise: your new understanding will help you to handle problems and create better relationships.

"Everyone's different" is also a truism for pregnancy and postpartum, andropause, peri and postmenopause, so keep communicating.

Please don't get annoyed when you see some version of this note repeated in all the chapters. I found some readers skipped this message and needed to be reminded.

# CHAPTER ONE

*"Fighter pilots are driven by testosterone. Every guy in the squadron thinks he is the Alpha male and the competition is non-stop. Who has the best gunnery scores? Who flies the best formation? Who is the smoothest flight lead? And who wins at darts in the lounge? Not all guys are so driven by their testosterone, however many do have the same tendencies whether it comes to their professional or their personal lives. "*

## TESTOSTERONE: THE BIG T

Testosterone, or the Big T as it is affectionately called, is the hormone that makes a man a man and is the basic reason why men can seem like alien creatures to women. And vice versa. When we understand what it does, we can compare it to our lover's hormones and see how the differences produce all those conflicts that drive us crazy and all those charms that keep us coming back for more.

Hormones play a decisive role in who and what we are, how we see the world and how we relate to each other. Amongst other things, our bodies produce these super fuels to help create growth, break down food for digestion and absorption, and most importantly, determine and shape our masculinity and femininity.

## MAKING A BOY

Despite a long history of husbands blaming their wives for not producing male heirs, it turns out that it's the sex chromosomes in men's sperm that determine their child's sex.

---

*NOTE» ALL UNFERTILIZED EGGS CARRY AN X CHROMOSOME. EACH SPERM CARRIES EITHER AN X (FEMALE) OR A Y (MALE) CHROMOSOME.*

---

If the Y fertilizes the egg, presto! It's a boy. The XY chromosome develops the embryo's male sex organs, which in turn release the T (testosterone) that shapes its masculinity. Likewise, if the X fertilizes the egg, you've got a girl. Her XX chromosome grows the female sex organs that release the estrogen that forms her femininity.

Let's say the Y sperm triumphs. After his sixth week, the boy's tiny testicles begin forming. They may be small, but they are mighty, going into overdrive and flooding his brain and body with testosterone. By his 16th week, he is producing as much T as he will as an adult. By his 24th week his T drops to the same amount he will have at early puberty.

What is all his testosterone doing? Building and destroying. All embryos are originally female. It takes focused and intensive work to transform that girl into a boy and T is the agent that makes it happen. Firstly, testosterone constructs the boy fetus' body, brain and the important brain circuits that run how males think, feel and act.

It also gets to work, along with another male hormone, *MIS*, to aggressively wipe out the female reproductive organs and inhibit brain circuits for feminine conduct. While cells in the communication area are destroyed and observation and emotional processing centers shrink, more cells in the sex and aggression centers are produced.

Some interesting questions to ponder are: What are the unconscious effects of that metamorphosis? Could all that effort to become a male make men innately resistant to feminizing influences? Is that why little boys generally agree that certain toys and games are for girls and reject them? Or make guys resist seeing "chick" flicks? Are they dismissing their lovers' suggestions to protect their manliness? Does anything feminine decrease their rank in the Alpha Male hierarchy? Or all of the above? Whatever the answers, Nature programmed males to adamantly create their masculinity.

All through his first year, our baby boy is energetically manufacturing those huge amounts of T to develop his male brain and male traits. Nature's primary directive is survival of the species and testosterone is programming these little men to do their part.

---

**NOTE**» MEN HAVE THE BIOLOGICAL MISSION
TO PROPAGATE, PROTECT AND PROVIDE.

---

For the next nine years, T decreases in what scientists call "juvenile pause."

## MAKING A MAN

Raging hormones mark the leap into manhood. Testosterone shoots up, so to speak, increasing ten times or more in puberty. As hormones surge again, penises grow, voices deepen, guys bulk up and start to shave. The sex circuits in their brain grow more than two times the size of a girl's. Overnight, females (or other males if they're gay) become intense objects of desire. Throughout men's lives, testosterone helps them get hard and produce sperm. It also contributes to the frequency and duration of their erections.

Both men and women need testosterone to maintain strength, mental and physical energy, bone density and muscle mass, and sex drive. But men have ten to one-hundred times more T circulating in their blood stream than ladies have in theirs, so guys often have a bigger sex drive and larger bodies, muscles and organs. Higher levels of testosterone are also linked to:

- *Wanting more sex*

- *Being more competitive*

- *Thinking in a more systemized way*

- *Being more dominant*

- *Being more aggressive*

- *Being more punishing*

- *Taking more risks*

- *Being more independent*

- *Being more singularly focused*

- *Being more action-oriented and less verbal*

- *Having increased spatial and mechanical abilities*

Testosterone increases the overall sense of well-being and self-esteem.

Low levels are linked to listlessness, depression and impotence.

## BOYS WILL BE BOYS

When women don't understand that "boys will be boys" they may want their men to want less sex and be less competitive, aggressive, dominant, risk-taking, and independent, etc. In other words, more like a woman, more like them. On the other hand, men might want women to see things more the way they do. These impractical wishes are probably the biggest underlying cause for the conflicts we see in couple's counseling. The sexes are simply not designed to work the same way.

## TESTOSTERONE AND SEX

Have you heard the jokes about men's English?

**May I have this dance? =**
**I'd eventually like to have sex with you.**

**Can I call you sometime? =**
**I'd eventually like to have sex with you.**

**Can I take you out to dinner? =**
**I'd eventually like to have sex with you.**

**Nice dress = Nice cleavage!**

**You look tense, let me give you a massage =**
**I want to fondle you.**

**What's wrong? =**
**I guess sex tonight is out of the question.**

**I love you = Let's have sex now!**

Sounds right to us. Unlike their lovers, guys are always thinking about sex and on the alert for sexual opportunities. The big T is the sex and aggression hormone for both sexes, but males' vastly higher amounts keep them focused on it. First of all, men create about 150 million sperm every day that are screaming to get out—and in and out and—never mind. Plus, testosterone is released into their bloodstreams every 17-60 seconds, fueling them with desire. What's a guy to do?

---

*NOTE» WOMEN GENERALLY THINK ABOUT SEX ONLY ONCE A DAY, OR WHEN THEY'RE HOTTEST, THREE OR FOUR TIMES A DAY.*

---

Their continual testosterone drip keeps men hungry for more. Foreplay to a male is a woman saying "yes." Built to inseminate as many women as possible to preserve humanity, they're armed and ready for action at the slightest provocation. That's why males are instinctively and obsessively on the lookout, especially for younger, potentially fertile females. Mentally undressing and fantasizing about the fair sex keeps their T going and thus, prepared. However, as beneficial as ogling other women might be to your sex drive, your lover could be turned off by it.

---

*NOTE» TO PREVENT HER FROM BEING INSULTED OR PISSED OFF, DO EVERYTHING YOU CAN TO CONCENTRATE ON HER WHEN YOU'RE TOGETHER.*

---

**❚❚***Doing exciting manly things also produces a flood of T. I can't tell you how many times I came back from an intense combat mission with an erection.* **❚❚**

---

**NOTE**» *FEMALES MAY NOT REALIZE THAT NATURE ENDOWED MALES WITH A NONSTOP DESIRE FOR SEX TO GUARANTEE SURVIVAL OF THE SPECIES, AND THUS MAY SEE IT AS A CHARACTER FLAW.*

---

They can especially perceive it that way if you're unfaithful or push sex with them when you haven't taken the trouble to turn them on.

## MORNING WOOD

Rise and shine and morning wood! Men are ready for sex the moment they wake up because their T levels are highest in the morning. Lucky is the man whose lover is also hot in the morning. You might not be him. Your partner could be like most women and not want you for breakfast. While some females might prefer you for lunch, many are lunar lovers, who are turned on in the evening when you're tired and ready to go to sleep. Oh well, you'll manage somehow.

## COMMITMENT

Then there's the casual sex vs. commitment conflict. That "inseminate everything that moves!" order generally makes it easier for men to separate sex from emotional attachment. Women's biological role as mothers makes Nature's command, "Find one man who will protect and provide for you and your kids" uppermost—even if she isn't planning to have kids. We talk about this clash of primal needs at length in our *Oxytocin: Love In The Sun* chapter.

## T TROUBLE

Males like testosterone charging them up because sexual energy is so powerful and feels great. But it can become burdensome and distracting to be dealing with sex all the time. How often do you feel like the little brain in your penis is overriding the big brain in your head? Has it ever damaged your judgment? Or diverted your attention from something important that needed to be done? Or got you into situations that cause BIG problems? The sex scandals of the rich and famous might make headlines, yet many of us can risk our relationships when our sex drive pilots the plane.

## BEING NUMBER ONE

Men compete for mates, ego, fun and survival. When you look at it, that's just about anything and everything. Whether it's winning a date with a luscious lady, a computer game, a Saturday morning baseball game or a job assignment, we can't help wanting to be the champ. Being the best and liking to be in control motivate us in a way that our more community-minded mates might not experience.

❚❚*I can't get in the car to drive to the grocery store without racing the guy in front of me. When I was flying it was about getting the best gunnery scores, or winning an air combat engagement. If I'm out for a day sailing I'm looking for ways to make the boat go faster so that when we race we can win. Winning makes me feel good, so I'm always looking for ways I can make that happen.* //

Glory isn't the only prize for victory: getting the gold has its biological rewards. When men (but not women) win at sports, their testosterone goes up and when they lose, it goes down. Ditto for their male fans whose T also rises if their favorite team wins, and lowers with a loss. Women wonder why sports can be such a serious, emotional issue to guys. But hey, it's not just a game when our T is on the line.

To the victor go the spoils and the winning edge. When testosterone is boosted, perception improves, focus sharpens and coordination is enhanced. Mood also gets better, and we become more confident, energetic, and willing to take more risks. All these physical and psychological advantages give us a better shot at succeeding again in our personal and career goals.

On the most primal level, beating the opposition means survival. Just as our sperm competes to get into the egg, we compete to get and keep our lover. Our ancestral fathers were rewarded for being the Alpha male by having females, lots of sex and attention, and strong, healthy kids who could survive brutal conditions. It also meant staying alive when enemies attacked.

On the romantic front, there is Paul J. Zak, the intrepid researcher, professor and author, who took blood tests of a bride, groom and all their guests before and after their wedding ceremony. Following the "I dos" everyone except the new husband had higher levels of oxytocin, the love and bonding hormone. Why didn't he? Because his T was one-hundred times his normal levels: he knew he had won the prize, big time.

So ladies, pass the chips and root for your partner's team to win, hope he'll come in first in his self-declared car race and understand this: so much of your man's competitive spirit is based, at its deepest unconscious level, on the importance of having a loving woman like you in his life.

## HIERARCHIES

Being Number One implies a hierarchy. Men are all about creating rigid linear systems with specific chains of command. We see it in governments, the military, corporations and religious institutions. Even sports have a team captain, head coach, leader boards and rankings.

Why do men crave that form of structure? One reason could be their Alpha male programming. Another is that research has found that the higher the prenatal T, the more systemized our thinking; the higher the prenatal oxytocin, the more empathetic we are. So, it's instinctual for males to both create hierarchies and to relate to having ladders to climb, seeing where they are in relation to others, and competing with them to get to the top rung. If the structure gets too suppressive, we rebel, but are often quick to put new belief systems and pecking orders in their place.

Females, who are usually the empathetic, high oxytocin ones, are on a completely different wavelength. Hierarchies are not their natural form of organization; women tend to thrive in groups that get input from its members and reach a consensus. Their drive to communicate and bond often puts them at odds with their partner's aggressive competition mode.

And historically, patriarchal chains of command have not been good to or for women, positioning them at the bottom of the pecking order and dismissing their non-T oriented input. There are tremendous social, economic and psychological repercussions to treating women this way, but we're not going to go into them or how things are or are not changing. Instead, we're focusing on the multitude of ways you and your mate's conflicting approaches play out in your love life. For example, your drive for status.

## STATUS

Nowadays, males usually use their brains rather than their brawn to compete for the power, authority, influence and resources to get to the top. While a guy might be crazy about his mate and/or their kids, he doesn't usually get his sense of purpose or self-esteem from his relationships. He needs a mission out in the world to motivate, challenge and define him and to give him standing. A man without such an objective usually feels lost, aimless and maybe worthless. That's why he pours his attention, endless hours and valuable energy into his work.

We've seen many a woman in couple's counseling who resented her mate's career mission because she felt he was neglecting her and/or the kids. Although career success was important to her, she made the relationship and family the priority. So, why couldn't he? Aside from her mate's whole pecking order/drive to compete and win mentality, a female's biology dictates "family first" and she usually derives her greatest pleasure and sense of self-esteem from healthy relationships. Much more about this in our next two chapters, *Estrogen: Women's Weather* and *Oxytocin: Love In The Sun*.

## DOES OUR STATUS MATTER TO WOMEN?

Absolutely. Despite the potential fallout from lack of attention, a man on a mission to achieve something and gain a high status is a major turn-on for women. So here's yet another reason why knowing who you are and identifying your mission are essential. Drive and ambition indicate T to spare and also promise financial survival. It's no surprise to anyone that the number one priority for women worldwide in choosing a mate is his ability to provide for her and their kids.

However, we live in a world of subcultures and more women are wage earners, so they might have other standards for who's on top. Depending on the group, being the smartest, the most talented, or the most aligned with her political or spiritual beliefs might give you high marks. Or she may have her own values that put you ahead of the competition—like supporting her ambitions, being kind, communicative, and wanting kids. Still, if you earn a living as well, you're probably unbeatable.

## LEADERSHIP VS. DOMINATION

▍▍*There are some important things to consider on our advance to being Number One: how we act on the way up and how we act when we get there. Some leaders subscribe to the 'Attila the Hun' approach, destroying everything and everyone who gets in their way and ruling by fear and intimidation.*

▍▍*Others follow the way of King Richard the Lion Hearted or Henry V, who led the famous band of brothers at Agincourt. These men were leaders who cared for their followers and made sure they were taken care of. They led by inspiration and example and ruled with justice and fairness. They knew that the privilege of leadership wasn't ego and power, but service.*

▍▍*There will always be bullies and tyrants, however they shouldn't be role models for success. Whether you're an officer in the Armed Services, a company boss, captain of your team or a father, you will find much more joy and be more effective if you govern by leadership rather than by terror and coercion.* **//**

---

**NOTE**» *IN TERMS OF PARENTING, IT SHOULD BE OBVIOUS THAT COMPETING WITH YOUR KIDS, ESPECIALLY YOUR SONS, TO BE THE ALPHA IS DAMAGING TO ALL CONCERNED.*

---

**//***I remember a great officer who taught me that in order to be a good leader you had to live by the motto: 'Never ask your men to do something you wouldn't do and do it first'. That doesn't always apply exactly but you get the idea. Another great axiom I learned was that 'practice bleeding is not a cost effective process'—for you or the troops you are leading.* **//**

## AGGRESSION

The noble vs. the suppressive leadership styles reflect the positive or negative sides of T and aggression.

---

**NOTE**» *THE HIGHER THE TESTOSTERONE, THE MORE AGGRESSIVE YOU ARE. ON THE CONSTRUCTIVE SIDE, THAT MEANS BEING MORE ASSERTIVE.*

---

**//***For example, when you put a fighter into a tight turn, you pull a lot of 'G' force.* **//**

---

**NOTE**» *THE FORCE OF GRAVITY IS 1 "G" FORCE.*

---

**❚❚** *3 to 4 G's is what pushes you down in your seat when you hit the bottom of a dive on a roller coaster. Aggressive fighter pilots love to pull at least 4 G tight turns. All fighter pilots are aggressive, but some more than others. When talking about a really aggressive fighter pilot, it is said that 'he pulls 6 G's just turning into the bathroom.'* **❚❚**

When we're being assertive, we have determination and energetically pursue our goals. It gives us the gas to win the point in a debate or basketball game, land the job, get the lady, or tackle a project with zest and get it done.

Moving on to the dark side; psychologically, aggression is defined as "hostile or violent behavior that is intended to cause harm or pain." Statistics show that men with high testosterone have higher levels of criminal violence.

---

***NOTE*»** *THE AGGRESSION CENTERS IN A MALE'S BRAIN ARE LARGER THAN IN A FEMALE'S.*

---

That's why it is so important to give teenage boys and young men healthy outlets and meaningful purposes. They've got all this newfound power coursing through them and they need the training and discipline to learn to control and focus it. Having mentors, working or playing on a team and identifying meaningful goals, help direct their awesome potential and teach them how to be valuable contributors to society.

## HAIR TRIGGER ATTACKS

One challenge guys might have to face on their path to being Warriors for The Good is controlling their spring-loaded tempers.

❚❚*Have you ever been in a situation where you suddenly lost your temper and Bam! Your anger shot up from zero to ten in a split second? Me too. There's a reason.* ❚❚

---

**WARNING**» WHEN A MAN GETS ANGRY, HIS T TRIGGERS THE AGGRESSION CENTER IN HIS BRAIN, MAKING HIM ANGRIER AND CAUSING A CHAIN REACTION.

---

When this happens, his increased anger boosts his T levels, which reactivate his aggression center and makes him even angrier, which in turn escalates his T until, BOOM! He explodes into rage. If we diagramed the cycle, it might look like this:

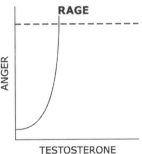

❚❚*It's hard to stop because our supersonic circuit works independently of the part of our brain that makes judgment. Road rage is a good example. The raping and pillaging that followed battles are also classic cases of*

testosterone gone wild, as are wife-beaters and rageaholics. It can cause havoc on the domestic front, as you may or may not have experienced. **//**

---

**CAUTION**» *EVEN IF IT ONLY HAPPENS ONCE IN A VERY LONG WHILE, IT CAN TERRORIZE YOUR MATE AND DAMAGE HER TRUST IN YOU AND HER SENSE OF SAFETY.*

---

**//** *But taking control is tricky: You only have a few seconds before you snap. However, I can often do it by recognizing the onset of anger before it escalates too much. You can try what I do:*

---

**CAUTION**» *THE INSTANT YOU SEE THAT YOU'RE GETTING ANGRY TAKE SOME DEEP BREATHS TO CHILL DOWN. IF YOU DO THIS QUICKLY ENOUGH, YOU MIGHT BE ABLE TO STOP THE VICIOUS CYCLE.*

---

**//** *Alternatively, before you explode or punch in a door, just walk away from a fight until you cool down.* **//**

It's vital for women to get this, so ladies:

---

**WARNING**» *IF YOU SEE YOUR MAN'S ANGER RAPIDLY RISING, STOP TALKING OR CALM HIM DOWN. IF HE TELLS YOU TO STOP TALKING, STOP. DO NOT EGG HIM ON.*

---

Also, ladies, let him walk away if he can't control his temper. We know this can be hard for you, because you might also be charged up. Even if you're right, the time to prove your point isn't when he's on the verge of detonating.

Plus, women are generally more capable of controlling the situation than men because of the difference in their brain wiring. Female's aggression and judgment centers are connected, so they can stop and think when they get angry and put on their brakes before they get violent. This is indispensable when you're dealing with crazy-making kids. Nature also thought it was a practical design because a cave woman losing control and provoking her bigger, stronger mate into a raging fury was a very, very bad idea. It still is.

Men, remember: Taking a time out doesn't mean you forget about the problem. Make a policy to set a specific time to talk about your issues later when both of you are more rational. If it can't be handled then and the issue is a core, recurring one, it's a good idea to go to couple's counseling. Ditto if the out-of-control anger is a pattern.

## BEING THE ENFORCER

Men are biologically programmed by their T to be less empathetic and more punishing to wrongdoers. Their mates, abundantly endowed with oxytocin, the bonding and empathy hormone, are programmed to be more forgiving.

---

**NOTE**» REMEMBER!
TESTOSTERONE **BLOCKS** OXYTOCIN.

---

Therefore, if a perceived transgression occurs, men are less likely to tolerate what they consider to be excuses or show mercy. What's good about that? On the home front, defiant kids might disregard mom's attempts to get them in line, but "wait till dad comes home" carries weight; they know he's a force to be reckoned with. As far as society goes, the same principle applies. Having physically strong, unsympathetic men who are wired to punish lawbreakers is, and always has been, a powerful deterrent to crime.

Slackers or lazy people can also instinctively raise men's ire. Prehistoric, tribal humans utterly depended on each other's contribution to secure the hard-earned food, resources and safety they needed to survive. The threat of pissed-off, T-primed, potentially violent men ensured that everyone pitched in.

Women, however, might not always agree with the way men enforce justice and boundaries. Rather, they can view it as being harsh, intolerant, and unforgiving. Guys in turn might disdain women's empathetic nature as being dangerously naïve, weak and enabling. This "too hard" vs. "too soft" gender conflict shows up in everything from politics to childrearing.

Whatever Nature wants, Nature gets. How do we know she wanted a balance between both ways of dealing with the world? Because she rewarded both empathy and enforcement activities with the same feel-good brain chemical, *dopamine.*

There's a lot more on the rewards of oxytocin in the *Oxytocin: Love In The Sun* chapter. Right now, here are three fascinating experiments that illustrate the chemical payoff men get for imposing penalties.

Paul J. Zak created a game to investigate the hormonal effects of trust or lack of it on the players. He soon discovered that the guys who felt cheated would hit back hard at the responsible participants. Blood samples of these ticked-off males revealed that *dihydrotestosterone* (*DHT*) the high-octane form of T had spiked. This is meaningful because DHT has a five-fold greater affect on the brain than plain old T, triggers aggressive actions, and increases pleasure-inducing dopamine when those deeds are done. None of the ladies had these reactions.

Paul J. Zak also had men play the game before and after applying a testosterone gel. The T-enhanced men doubled their rate of punishment. In another experiment, non-cooperative game players were zapped with mild electroshocks. When males, but not the females, observed it, two brain areas were affected: the dopamine rich ones were activated and those connected to pain were deactivated.

---

*NOTE» THE HIGHER THE T, THE MORE PUNISHING THE MEN WERE!*

---

It may sound sadistic for men to be chemically rewarded for teaching others a lesson, but being an umpire in the game of life can be very dangerous when you're dealing with Al Qaeda, tyrants, drug lords and other criminals. It helps to have good feelings when you're protecting society from them.

The obvious flaw in the design is that determining what's right or wrong can be very subjective. The movies are spot-on when they show the villains getting even and enjoying it. Plus, ideologies, religions, nations, political parties and cultures create their own sets of prejudices and rules. How many wars were "just"? Was the inquisition? Slavery? The Holocaust? All were gaily enforced by their adherents. And what about the denial of civil rights to women and minorities that continues in various forms and in different societies to this day?

In their relationships, females are commonly punished for unwarranted jealousy, not doing what controlling men want, or doing the exact same thing their double-standard men do. The penalty can be physical, emotional or financial. The majority of those who live below the poverty line have always been women and children, thanks to dead-beat exes and dads.

Hence, T's directive to enforce the rules that safeguard society must be used with wise discernment. "Do no harm to the innocent, the women and the children" is central to the "Warriors Code of Honor" and to fighting for what is right.

## TAKING MORE RISKS

❚❚*There's a military anecdote about asking for volunteers to clean up the camp; no one volunteered, but when asked to volunteer for a dangerous, life-threatening mission, all the hands went up. Why? Pushing their limits and taking risks is how men discover who they are and what they're capable of doing.* ❚❚

---

**NOTE**» THIS WAS BEFORE WOMEN
SERVED IN THE ARMED FORCES.

---

Would women choose to go on a dangerous mission? Our guess is that they would offer their services out of a sense of duty rather than for the thrill of doing it. Both male's and female's responses to taking risks are directly tied to their relationship to *cortisol,* the stress hormone. High levels of cortisol produce caution and protectiveness. If the levels are low or are blocked, people are prone to take more risks. Which hormone do you think obstructs it?

---

**NOTE**» TESTOSTERONE BLOCKS CORTISOL.

---

❚❚*Teenage boys and young men have the highest levels of testosterone. That's when they feel immortal and do crazy stunts. The rational, thinking part of their brain isn't fully developed until the early 20s. So, loaded with testosterone and not able to think things through, they could literally be all balls and no brain. I don't know about you, but this explains a lot about my teenage years.* **//**

On the positive side, their T-blocking cortisol gives men the courage to be bolder and face terrifying adversaries, like dinosaurs and bigger guys on the basketball court.

**//** *There are countless examples of fighter pilots dueling with anti-aircraft guns. This is definitely a high risk, life-or-death venture. It happened day after day on the Ho Chi Minh trail, where Vietcong AA guns were protecting their major supply line to the South. They had to be silenced in order for US attack bombers to come in and bomb the supply lines.*

**//** *The anti-aircraft battery positions were very small, only 25-30 feet across and were sunk in a pit or surrounded with sand bags. It took a direct hit with a bomb to destroy one. So, while the Vietcong were shooting at them, the pilots needed to roll in to bomb it, and then straighten out to get a good bomb release. The anti-aircraft guns could track and shoot them down before they had a chance to release their bombs. The shells whizzing by were distracting and could mess up the pilot's aim so it was hard to for them hit their target. Too often, the Vietcong AA gun won.*

**//** *Even though we knew the odds, we didn't think about the risk/benefit in attacking an AA gun. With our testosterone blocking our cortisol, our focus was on the challenge, winning and accomplishing our mission.* **//**

## WHY ARE WOMEN SO RISK-AVERSE?

You're all ready to race your car on a wet, slippery track and your partner is listing ten reasons why you shouldn't. You think she's a worrywart. She thinks you're reckless. You chant the male mantra "everything will be okay." She checks your will to make sure she's still the beneficiary.

---

**NOTE**» ESTROGEN ELEVATES CORTISOL,
MAKING FEMALES MORE CAUTIOUS
AND PROTECTIVE.

---

Nature balanced out your tendency to take chances by designing your lover to be the careful, guarded one. In early civilization, it was up to the woman to make sure that her family didn't eat poisoned vegetation, that the kids didn't adopt the orphaned baby tyrannosaurus as a pet and that her mate didn't impetuously decide to go hunting in a blinding ice storm. It's more or less the same today. The ladies are usually prone to play it safe in everything from safe sex to how they deal with money, and especially how they care for their kids.

A typical running battle in childcare can pit dad against mom.

*To him: she's overprotective, coddling the kids and making them weak.*

*To her: he has a reckless disregard for danger or consequences.*

Parents may come together in white-knuckled agreement, however, after they witness the harrowing choices their teenagers are making.

Men also take more physical risks because they're larger, more muscular and testosterone mutes physical pain: think football or bull riding. Estrogen, on the other hand, makes the fair sex more sensitive to pain.

## INDEPENDENCE

Stubborn independence is a T-driven character-istic that your partner may consider foolhardy, but you prize as a hallmark of your intelligence. For example: You have a question about an item on your taxes. Your mate suggests calling your accountant and asking her what to do. You think: "What a stupid idea!" Why would you waste your time on a three-minute call when you can get the very same answer yourself in three hours?

**❙❙** *In my case, I love to tinker, build things and play with my tools. If I attempt a fairly complicated project, I will screw it up three times rather than ask an expert how to do it. When I built my racecar, I had a stack of parts that didn't quite work in the corner and a ton of satisfaction.* **❙❙**

Take note, ladies: time is not of the essence in these male-learning exercises. T drives your partner to act indepen-dently, to constantly test and prove to himself that he can do "it." Achieving whatever "it" is on his own is very gratifying and gives him a sense of self-worth. He's also demonstrating his power since what he does personally shows other people his particular value.

This DIY (Do-It-Yourself) mentality is the total opposite from the female's community minded "input and help from all" frame of mind.

## SINGLE-FOCUSED AND ON A MISSION

Men like to set a goal and concentrate on doing one thing at a time to accomplish their missions. We talked about missions before in the context of life purposes, but here we're talking about tasks big or small. It could be a complicated job at work or a simple fix-it task at home. It doesn't matter. A mission is a mission.

A guy tends to get upset when something is put in the way of completing his designated mission. If someone, let's say his lover, wants to talk to him while he's focused on finishing a task, such as reading the sports page, he could get very annoyed. The conversation that follows, if one does, probably won't be very enjoyable.

▍▍*Being single-focused can have its downside. Have you been very excited about a new mission and couldn't wait to get started, but about half way to two thirds through it, couldn't wait to be finished? That's when being tired of being on the same project sets in and you just want to get it DONE and move on to something else. It can be tempting to rush the job, even though you may not do your best work.*

**❚❚** *Women are multitaskers. They can seamlessly work on diverse projects or tasks at the same time: chat on the phone, cook breakfast, check the email and dress the kids. As a man I look at this and wonder how they ever get anything done. But they do. And they don't get bored—overwhelmed maybe—but not bored.* **❚❚**

Have you noticed that females can also talk and drive, and might expect you to? Worse, they could get upset when you can't. Both experiences are very aggravating.

---

**NOTE**» *LADIES, IF YOUR MATE IS FOCUSING ON NAVIGATING TRAFFIC, HE CAN'T PROCESS ANYTHING—ESPECIALLY IF IT'S IMPORTANT, EMOTIONAL OR HE NEEDS TO REMEMBER IT. SAVE IT FOR LATER.*

---

Men, if your partner is not reading this, share or explain men's need to concentrate on one thing at a time. Then make what should be your new, standard policy when you can't discuss something right away: setting a specific time to talk about it later. And don't forget to add how much you love her.

## ACTION OVER WORDS

Women adore hearing words of affection, but it might not be natural for their men to say them. Your lover's brain and hormones specifically equip her to observe, listen and verbally communicate. Additionally, the emotional center of her brain is connected to her verbal centers, making it easy for her to express her feelings.

In general, men prefer to do something rather than talk about it. Being still and patiently listening is hard for many men, as is being in touch with and articulating their emotions. To prove that he loves her, a man will buy his baby gifts, do things around the house, and run errands for her but he will rarely tell her how much he loves her or how beautiful he thinks she is. He's under the misconception that his actions speak for him.

Guys have been known to grumble about gals expecting them to read their minds. Well, your mate can't read yours either. She can get really excited about dressing up and looking fine in that tight black dress with the cleavage plunging just for you. If you don't compliment her, she'll get bummed out because she'll assume you didn't notice or aren't impressed—even if you do spend $150 for dinner. Ditto in the affection department. To her, slaving away at a job doesn't replace a sincere declaration of appreciation. It's more important still after you've been together for a while, or when she becomes a mom.

---

**NOTE**» *AND LADIES, YOU MIGHT NEED TO USE YOUR REMARKABLE OBSERVATIONAL SKILLS TO SEE THAT YOUR MAN IS MAKING NON-VERBAL DECLARATIONS OF LOVE. HE TOO DESERVES TO BE ACKNOWLEDGED.*

---

Two of the assignments we give couples is to take time every day to list all the things they value about their partner and to learn to say "thank you" after each helpful or loving act. It may take a while to rewire their brains to focus on the positive, but if they work at it, mutual gratitude and a happy relationship become the norm.

## SPATIAL/MECHANICAL ABILITIES

Lastly, and actually the least important characteristic in terms of your love life, is men's spatial/mechanical skills. Still, we've got to include them for insight into the male psyche.

Prenatal testosterone grows the spatial/mechanical regions in male brains, which endows them with the innate ability to operate in three-dimensional space. Why is that so important? For the usual reason: survival of the species. Our ancestral brothers had to be able to hurl their spears and hit fierce, fast-moving animals to protect and feed both their families and themselves. They also needed to navigate large expanses of land in search of game and recall how to get home with it. Today, we use those hard-wired aptitudes in throwing a ball though a hoop while running, playing video games or in estimating volume and spatial relationships in architecture and civil engineering.

---

*NOTE»* *MOST GAMES MEN CREATED*
*AND LOVE TO PLAY USE THEIR SPATIAL*
*AND MECHANICAL TALENTS: BASEBALL,*
*BASKETBALL, FOOTBALL, SOCCER, RUGBY,*
*HOCKEY, VOLLEYBALL TENNIS, GOLF, POLO,*
*ARCHERY, DARTS, ETC.*

---

❚❚ *Flying is another example. Pilots must be able to maneuver an airplane, change speeds, direction and altitude in order to land the airplane on the precise spot. And when it comes to spatial/mechanical skills, we're frickin' multi-tasking geniuses. Fly the airplane, read the map, talk on the radio, plan the weapons delivery, analyze target defenses, put the bomb on the target and avoid the ground fire in the area. Piece o' cake.* ❚❚

Ladies, have you ever freaked out when you thought your partner was driving too close and was going to hit another car? Rest assured, he probably wasn't. He sees spatial relationships better than you do, especially at night. That ability also makes it easier for him to park.

## DETERMINING FACTORS

Of course we could say a lot more about what T does, but we think you've got a good working understanding of it by now. So we're moving on to another important part of the

47

testosterone dynamic: the conditions that influence *how much* you have.

To begin with, your genes establish your initial amount of T; the more you have, the more your brain will be shaped by it and the more T traits you'll demonstrate.

---

**NOTE**» *MOST MEN FALL MID-RANGE ON THE TESTOSTERONE GRAPH.*

---

High, low or medium, T peaks in males in their late teens and early 20s, then gradually declines by 1%-2% a year. As it goes, so goes T-dependent behavior, reducing your sex drive, combativeness, risk-taking, etc. By the time you reach middle age, you might start having the discomforting realization that you are not who you used to be. It's an important subject, and our *Andropause: Male Climate Change* chapter is devoted to the symptoms you might experience and the adjustments you might need to make.

Your T is also predictably tuned to the seasons. You might imagine that spring fever and steamy summer nights would be when your T would rise. However, a study of 44,000 male veterans proved that levels go up in the winter and fall—exactly like our primate cousins.

Besides age and the natural rhythm of the seasons, there are the fluctuating levels of T we talked about when men look at women, fantasize or are turned on by someone. But it doesn't take a special occasion or a special woman to boost T.

Nature, in its infinite quest for babies, increases it by the mere presence of a woman, *any* woman; she doesn't even have to be attractive. One experiment found that men's T rose 7% after being with a woman for five minutes, and even more if they had high T levels to begin with.

Can you guess what happens if you are actually on the prowl for sex? Right. Up it goes—the testosterone, that is. That's why single and cheating men both have higher levels. When does it go down? When you're courting, committed or married, making it easier for you to connect deeply with your partner. T decreases even more when you become a dad, plunging by a third in the first few weeks after your child is born.

When does it go back up? After a breakup or a divorce when it is time to find a new lover.

## THE HIGH-T MAN

Usually the successful high-T men are "A" types who embody all the testosterone traits, but amped way up; for example, many CEOs, trial lawyers, top athletes, politicians, fighter pilots and racecar drivers. We idealize high-T men in stories and films as the Alpha male warriors, super heroes who can confront and defeat anyone and anything. In our fantasies, we'd like to be them. In real life, maybe not so much.

Many high-T men do have the energy, drive and ethics to accomplish great things and have great relationships.

Having an abundance of testosterone, however, doesn't guarantee success. Without the proper instruction, guidance and self-discipline, high–T men can suffer from uncontrolled aggression, inability to deal with frustration and irrational risk-taking. They also have a higher percentage of criminal violence, unemployment and suicide.

And while some of our superheroes get laid, they don't usually have great relationships. Statistically, high-T men marry less, have more affairs, divorce and hit their wives more.

## THE LOW T MAN

Genetically low testosterone men have fewer T characteristics and more estrogen and oxytocin attributes, such as: being more in touch with emotions, verbal, nurturing, community oriented, etc.

Even if your T levels are normal, illness, street or medical drugs can decrease them. How would you know? Is your once active libido low? Are you tired? Depressed? Or all three? Fortunately, modern medicine can test to determine if you have the condition called *Low T* and can prescribe testos-terone replacement treatment to restore your levels.

---

**NOTE**» *KEEP THIS IN MIND, ESPECIALLY FROM YOUR EARLY 50'S ON, WHEN THESE SYMPTOMS MIGHT APPEAR.*

---

## WOMEN AND THE BIG T

Testosterone plays a major role in female eroticism, driving women's lust, arousal, pleasure and orgasm. This "hormone of desire" ensures that her nipples and clitoris become erect and sensitive to touch.

---

**NOTE**» YOUR LOVER'S ENTIRE VAGINAL AREA IS MADE UP OF ERECTILE TISSUE AND, JUST LIKE YOUR PENIS, NEEDS TO BE ENGORGED WITH BLOOD FOR HER TO ORGASM.

---

Which brings us to the all-important question: "When is she hottest?" It's probably no surprise that young women in their early 20s have the most T. After that, like it does with guys, it gradually declines. Sadly, unlike guys, the ladies aren't ready to jump into bed at any time.

Unless they've just fallen madly in love or are sex-starved, pre-menopausal women's sex drive is controlled by their menstrual cycle. Testosterone goes up in the second week of the cycle and peaks when they ovulate—meaning she's hot AND fertile—just the way Nature intended. It declines in the last two weeks, lowering her sex drive and the power of her orgasms. You're moments away from reading about it in detail in our next chapter, *Estrogen: Women's Weather.*

## LADIES IN LOVE

You've found the girl of your dreams and you're in love. There's romance, passion and marathon sex—just the way you like it. Finally a woman's libido matches yours. Enjoy it while you can, for this too shall pass. Just as your T levels lower in courtship, enabling you to be more open to talking, listening, and being emotional, your love-struck partner's testosterone rises, making her hornier. Nature knows what it takes to get us hooked up. After the hot, romantic, bonding courtship stage ends, you and your lover are both back to normal—in your hormone levels, sex drive and ways of communicating and relating.

## THE HIGH-T WOMAN

---

**NOTE**» *THERE IS JUST AS MUCH DIFFERENCE BETWEEN HIGH AND LOW TESTOSTERONE WOMEN AS THERE IS BETWEEN HIGH AND LOW TESTOSTERONE MEN.*

---

You see a 5'2", 105 lb. wisp of a woman and think "what a delicate little thing." If you got to know her and she was a high-T woman, you'd discover that she was about as fragile as a lioness.

Gals with high testosterone have the same characteristics as high-T guys. This petite pistol would have a big sexual appetite, be a more ambitious, aggressive competitor, take more risks, smile less, and have more affairs than her lower-T girlfriends.

## T AND CHEMISTRY

So you have this high–T sexpot. Does that mean you want to have a relationship with her? If you're a high-T male, probably not. And vice versa. Who wants to come home and aggressively compete with their mate? Consequently, high-T males and females are often attracted to and happier with more nurturing partners. And their lower-T partners are turned on by their mate's boldness and energy.

Nature intended opposites to attract so couples would have all the survival bases covered. But it's not as simple as high and low testosterone. Everyone's different and chemistry is complex, so there's no one formula for who turns you on and who you want to be with. Add cultural and social needs. But, basically males and females are attracted to partners who *complement their energy and behavior rather than duplicate them*. Which means that there really is someone for everyone, be it macho or sensitive man or anyone in between.

## T AND OTHER HORMONES IN WOMEN

Men frequently note that they are simpler and easier to read than their lovers. They have a point. Although guys are influenced by the same hormones as women, T generally rules. Not so with the fair sex. Nature has fueled them with a complex mix of estrogen, progesterone and oxytocin that creates those complementary, but often challenging attitudes and drives. Luckily guys love to test themselves and so are up to meeting the challenge. Our next two chapters explain how those mystifying women work, which should be a big help in your love, sex and relationship life.

This chart can also help clarify how testosterone works and influences men and women.

## THE TESTOSTERONE CHART

| TESTOSTERONE |
|:---:|
| ***BIOLOGY*** |
| Floods brain in womb making male brain |
| Forms the male sex organs |
| Surges in puberty |
| Creates the male secondary sex characteristics |
| Responsible for erections |
| Contributes to frequency and duration of erections |
| Men have 10-100xs more circulating in their blood stream |
| ***HEALTH*** |
| Maintains strength |
| Maintains mental and physical energy |
| Maintains bone density |
| ***IN SEX*** |
| Responsible for sex drive |
| Releases into men's blood stream every 17-60 seconds |
| Makes men think about sex |

| TESTOSTERONE |
| --- |
| In men, highest levels in the morning |
| Drive for casual sex with many partners |
| Don't need foreplay |
| *COMPETITION* |
| Competitive drive to win |
| T higher if males win, lower if they lose |
| T doesn't rise or fall if women win or lose |
| T rising gives better perception, focus and coordination |
| *DOMINANCE* |
| Drive to dominate and win |
| Drive to be the Alpha male |
| Drive to get and keep high social status |
| Hierarchal |
| *AGGRESSION* |
| The higher the testosterone, the more aggressive |
| Hair trigger response to anger in men |
| *ENFORCER* |
| Tendency to punish perceived wrongdoers |
| The higher the T the greater the desire to punish |
| Experiences pleasure in punishing |
| *RISK* |
| The higher the T levels, the greater the risk-taking |
| T blocks cortisol, the stress hormone |

| TESTOSTERONE |
|:---:|
| ***SINGLE FOCUS*** |
| Higher T, more singularly focused |
| Mission-oriented |
| ***SPEECH*** |
| Prenatal T blocks the language centers in the brain |
| Less verbal |
| Action oriented |
| ***SPATIAL/MECHANICAL SKILLS*** |
| Prenatal T develops spatial/mechanical parts of the brain |
| ***INDEPENDENCE*** |
| Drive for personal, independent action |
| Drive for space |
| Focus on mission |

# THE TESTOSTERONE QUIZ

Here's a quiz for men and women that helps you rate how much T you have. Have your mate take it, too, and compare. It's very enlightening.

**Rate your answers on the following scale:**

Almost Never = 1
Rarely = 2
Sometimes = 3
Often = 4
Almost Always =5

1. My sex drive is very strong. _____
2. I am very competitive. _____
3. I want to be the leader or the boss. _____
4. I am very aggressive. _____
5. I like taking risks. _____
6. I prefer action to talking. _____
7. I like to do it by myself. _____
8. I like to focus on doing one thing at a time. _____
9. I'm very comfortable working in a hierarchal system. _____
10. I'm more mission-oriented than relationship-oriented. _____

**TOTAL** _____

**If you scored:**

40-50, you are very influenced by testosterone.
10-20, you are minimally influenced by testosterone.
21-39, you are in the middle range.

# CHAPTER TWO

❝The thing about being a professional pilot—military or civilian—is that you have to fly when you are supposed to fly, no matter what the weather. Flying jets, which rapidly cover a lot of territory, exposes you to constantly changing weather. Sometimes it can transform very quickly, the storms in winter in the northern latitudes and the sudden thunderstorms in the south during summer are especially abrupt.

❝I'll never forget my first night solo formation flight in the F100. It was supposed to be a simple formation take off and short navigation flight, back in about one hour. The weather was really bad. Cloud ceilings and visibility were just *high enough to allow flying and it was raining hard. There was no radar in the F100 so we wound up flying through one thunderstorm after another.*

*\\There was nothing to do but tuck it in close, overlap the wings so that I didn't lose sight of the leader and work the stick, rudder and throttle for all that I was worth. We always got a weather briefing before we flew so we knew we were in for a ride. When I landed, my flight suit was soaked with sweat.*

*\\It helps when you know what the weather is. You can plan for it; maybe go around it or over it. Sometimes you just have to go through it and deal with it. If you have radar you can see the areas of heaviest precipitation and fly around it. If there are icing conditions, you for sure want to avoid that. If there are extreme conditions like hurricanes, or tornadoes, you just don't go there. //*

# ESTROGEN: WOMEN'S WEATHER

## VARIABLE WEATHER

You have undoubtedly noticed that your woman's emotions change a lot more than yours do: sunny, stormy, clear skies, partially cloudy, sunlit again, rain. It can happen in a day or at different times of her monthly cycle. Sometimes you know how to fly through them, and sometimes you're flying blind.

As her moods change, so do her thoughts and actions. What's good is now bad, like your relationship. Decisions can also fluctuate: you're supposed to go to a movie at five o'clock, but now it's four o'clock and she feels like going for a bike ride instead.

*To him: a decision is a conclusion.*

*To her: it's more like an option—especially if it's before an event and involves clothes.*

You may have seen "The Female Rules." Two that pertain are:

**1. The Female can change her mind at any time.**

**2. The Male must never change his mind without the express written consent of The Female.**

It takes a courageous and skillful man to successfully navigate the varying atmospheric conditions of his lady's many moods.

## WHY DO WOMEN CHANGE SO MUCH?

Women are built to feel deeply and to respond to life's joys, sorrows and stresses with a broad range of emotions. Their fluctuating hormones, however, add a whole other physical dimension to the mix.

The climate is fairly predictable for men because of that steady drip of testosterone entering their blood streams. Age and certain events affect their T, but their sex drives, moods, self-esteem and abilities aren't affected by daily variations in levels. Not so for females of childbearing age whose estrogen, progesterone and testosterone are constantly changing in amounts and in ratio to each other; thus the shifting weather.

Estrogen (E) and progesterone are the two major female sex hormones and are mainly produced in your partner's ovaries. These two super-fuels surge in puberty, then rise and fall monthly during her menstrual cycles. Up and down her hormones go and up and down your woman goes mentally, physically and emotionally.

Your mate's E and progesterone levels yoyo until she stops producing 80% of them in postmenopause. Pregnancy, postpartum (after childbirth) blues and peri (around) menopause are also times when her hormones dramatically rise and fall, ushering in unpredictable weather and a whole new set of challenges.

This chapter takes a close look at how your partner's monthly cycles influence her—and the effects that might have on you and your relationship. But before we go there, here are some basics about E that you should know.

## MAKING A GIRL

Estrogen makes the girl. Both male and female fetuses are flooded by their mother's estrogen in the womb, but as you've read, boys produce huge amounts of T to neutralize it. It's the inundation from her mom, not the small amount of E from her tiny ovaries that forms a girl's body, brain and brain circuits. Since her estrogen isn't suppressed, her cells are free to happily grow those hallmarks of a female brain: her mighty observation, communication and emotional processing centers.

A few months after birth, the infant girl's ovaries start producing the same amount of estrogen she will produce in puberty. Why? Nature doesn't manufacture unisex models. It wants to make sure this female differs mentally, emotionally and physically from a male—survival of the species, mothering and all that.

For the next 24 months, those massive amounts of estrogen continue to flood the girl toddler's body and brain, reinforcing and developing her femininity. Then "juvenile pause" takes over and down her estrogen goes.

## MAKING A WOMAN

The Big E surges again in puberty, turning that little girl into a young woman. Her ovaries, uterus and vagina mature, making her able to conceive. At the same time, her secondary sex characteristics—those defining traits that don't relate to reproduction—cause young men to go on alert. Almost overnight, her pelvis widens, her body fat increases giving her newly curvaceous hips, an admirable butt and lovely breasts.

As impressive as these transformations are, the most radical shift for a teenage girl is getting her period. Teenage boys experience tricky changes in puberty, but they don't compare with their girlfriends' monthly cycles. It's not just the bleeding with its potential discomfort or even pain, which is a huge deal all on its own; it can also have tough emotional and psychological challenges. This is when weather reports really come in handy.

When a woman is ready to conceive, her estrogen:

- *Regulates her periods*

- *Helps her have a nicely lubricated, supple and slippery vagina for easy entrance*

- *Produces the mucous in her cervix which affects how long sperm lives*

- *Prepares the uterus for pregnancy by enriching and thickening the lining*

> **NOTE**» THERE ARE 3 MAIN KINDS OF
> ESTROGEN A WOMAN PRODUCES. DURING
> HER FERTILE YEARS, ESTRADIOL DOMINATES.
> WHEN WE SAY "ESTROGEN" IN THIS CHAPTER,
> WE'RE TALKING ABOUT ESTRADIOL. WE'LL
> BE TALKING ABOUT THE TWO OTHERS IN THE
> PREGNANCY AND MENOPAUSE CHAPTERS.

## WHAT ELSE DOES ESTROGEN DO?

The brain is the command central and regulates everything the body does. Your mate's copious E affects all her brain cells—from how they're structured and hooked up to the electrical connections between them. What's the impact? Huge. Amongst other things, it affects her:

- *Cognition*

- *Learning*

- *Memory*

- *Mood*

- *Communication*

- *All her organs*

- *300 different tissues in her body*

- *Weight*

- *Sleep*

E also makes her:

- *Heart healthy*

- *Bones stronger*

- *Hair glossy*

- *Skin moist and radiant*

- *Sensitive to touch*

- *Experience sexual pleasure*

- *Have a stronger libido*

- *Orgasmic*

Through the remainder of her fertile years and for the rest of her life, the way your partner experiences the world, mentally, emotionally and physically, will in large part be shaped by her E or lack of it.

## WHY IS SHE SO EMOTIONAL?

Remember those three brain processing centers that her E created that make her so different from you? Observation + emotion + communication = an emotional brain machine that is geared to talk about what she sees. Plus she has fluctuating amounts of E constantly fueling it. This also explains her gift of gab.

## EMOTIONAL RADAR

*To you: someone crying or angry communicates loud and clear.*

*To her: any little thing on a person's face signals something's right or wrong.*

While this ability to observe what's going on with you or the kids might seem almost psychic to you, it's as ordinary as breathing to your partner. For example, you might be talking to your lover and she asks: "What's wrong?" You, of course, say: "Nothing." She says "you look upset" and persists in trying to probe how you're really feeling. Not only do you not feel upset, but she's beginning to piss you off. You might feel like she's probing when you don't feel like being probed. It's only hours later that you realize she's right: you ARE upset about a problem at work. How does she know?

Nature gave your mate her innate ability to read emotions and hear the different tones of voice because she had to understand the needs of infants who couldn't speak. She also had to protect herself and her kids from powerfully built cave men who might fly off the handle.

All this would be well and good if it weren't for the fact that your lover expects you to do the same. Are you ever shocked by her sudden fury/hurt/withdrawal/crying? What you subsequently discover is that she's been upset for days. You didn't have a clue. Why didn't she tell you there was a problem? Are you supposed to read her mind? Well, yes. As far as your lover is concerned, it couldn't have been more obvious: it was written all over her face and expressed in the tone of her voice. Her conclusion: you didn't give a damn. A horrible fight and endless processing to follow.

---

**CAUTION**» *SORRY, LADIES, YOU'RE GOING TO HAVE TO SAY WHAT'S GOING ON, OUT LOUD, IN WORDS. OTHERWISE, HE PROBABLY WON'T GET IT.*

---

And guys, if you have the slightest inkling something's wrong, ask—even if it means talking about it then and there. It will be far less painful, we promise. Better a shower than a thunderstorm.

## EMOTION CENTRAL

A tremendous amount of emotional traffic whirrs around in your partner's pretty brain. It's a result of her much more powerful emotional center and the larger and more active nerve routes to and from it. The constant gathering and processing of emotional information is how your mate experiences and deciphers the world around her. Above and beyond any verbal content, she wants to know: "What am I feeling?" "What are you feeling?' "What is my girlfriend feeling?" "What is the stranger across the room feeling?" Her emotional curiosity is boundless. Understanding how she and others feel enables her to connect and relate to them. Her emotions give her the valuable information about people and situations she needs to set goals, make decisions and solve problems.

---

**NOTE**» *LADIES: WHEN YOUR MAN SAYS HE DOESN'T KNOW HOW HE FEELS, HE'S NOT BEING EVASIVE OR STUPID. HE'S JUST GOT OTHER MACHINERY AND TALENTS.*

---

On the lighter side, her emotional aptitudes also play a part in the conflict over which movie or TV show to watch. Whereas your T drives you to action, your mate's E drives her to character-driven entertainment. You might find her choices boring because "nothing's happening." Meanwhile, she's riveted to the greatly satisfying world of action she sees on the actors' faces. Oh well. Time to compromise and take turns choosing.

## WEATHER REPORTS

No! Your mate will not get to the point!

*To him: communication is a destination. Getting to the point is the point.*

*To her: communication is a journey in which she moves from one thought to another, eventually weaving them together into an intricate and complete answer—which you might or might not understand. Underlying it all, and possibly more important than the ideas, are the emotions she feels each step of the way.*

Although you might not be able to track your partner's route, there are people who can: her girlfriends. Have you ever watched them in action? There they sit, enmeshed in conversation, exploring each other's thoughts and emotions, reading small nuances in the tones of their voices and in slight changes of expression, and going deeper and deeper. Paradise to them. Maybe hell to you.

## WHY DOESN'T SHE EVER FORGET?

**A married man should forget his mistakes—there's no use in two people remembering the same thing.**

Ah, the legendary female memory: the once recorded, never forgotten ammo to be used in all arguments proving that you, once again, have screwed up.

*To him: Emotional memory is like the RAM that gets erased when we turn our computers off.*

*To her: Emotional memory is like the hard drive that stores everything forever.*

Why? Because her abundant flow of natal estrogen also built a memory storage system in her brain that is both larger than yours and rich in estrogen receptors. With her plentiful E fueling it, she has been given an awesome ability to collect, file and retrieve information from an ever-growing database.

She will be particularly able to recall emotionally charged incidents and to articulate her arguments like a seasoned prosecutor because her memory brain circuits are connected to her emotional and verbal centers. Yours are not. So, be good. Be very, very good. Hopefully, she'll remember that too, but you may have to remind her.

## UPS AND DOWNS

Your mate's ability to observe, communicate verbally, and remember goes up and down with her E levels. When she has the right amount, she's up and confident. When she has too much or too little, you run into cloudy weather.

---

**NOTE**» *TOO LITTLE E LEADS TO DEPRESSION, ANXIETY, AND VARIOUS KINDS OF CRAVING DISORDERS. TOO MUCH E LEADS TO MOOD SWINGS, DEPRESSION AND HEALTH PROBLEMS.*

---

Moreover, estrogen is also interacting with progesterone and testosterone, so there's an intricate balancing act playing out in your woman's body all of the time. If her hormones are harmonious, so are her emotions; if her hormones are out of whack, so it will be with her emotions. When might you encounter these difficulties? During PMS, pregnancy, after birth, and in peri and postmenopause.

## WEATHER FACTORS

*Serotonin*, the feel good, calming brain chemical is another big player in your mate's shifting weather. The more serotonin, the more positive and happy we feel and the more pleasure we experience. (Lucky you, men have more.) As it happens, E and serotonin are co-dependent. When your partner's estrogen falls, so does her serotonin, making her feel down and anxious; when her E comes back up—like at the

71

beginning of her period—her serotonin rises, the sun comes out and she's calm again.

As you will learn in the *Oxytocin: Love In The Sun* chapter, oxytocin is also intimately entwined with your woman's weather. It impacts everything from her need to bond, spend time, and communicate with you, to her levels of trust, stress and, as pointed out in The Big T, empathy.

## HIGH ESTROGEN WOMEN

While testosterone makes a woman hotter, estrogen makes her juicier. The more E, the more fertile a woman is and the more you are instinctively drawn to her like a heat seeking missile. Nature also endowed the high-E female with a prettier face, making the "I'm fertile" announcement loud and clear. This high-E babe also looks younger, and according to researcher Kristine Durante, Ph.D., dresses more provocatively and has more sex.

Even if you hit the target and have a relationship with this beauty, she may or may not keep you. Dr. Durante also found that the high-E woman knows she's desirable and has lots of choices, so she has very high mating standards. She wants you to have the best genes, be good in bed and be a good provider. Thus she's more likely to cheat or trade up, if what she considers to be a higher quality mate, arrives on the scene.

A universally common problem is that the more T you have, the more you're attracted to women with high-E levels. While that's hot in terms of chemistry, "opposites attract" doesn't imply getting along well with each other. With conflicting needs and psychology, the "war between the sexes" has a certain inevitability. That is, unless you understand, tolerate and enjoy the differences, which is why you're reading this book, right?

## PROGESTERONE

*Progesterone* is the other main hormone produced in the ovaries of menstruating women. It's the "promotes gestation hormone." Whereas estrogen and testosterone help our ladies conceive, progesterone:

- *Helps them sustain the progress of the pregnancy*
- *Helps to makes a nice, cushiony nest for the fertilized egg to grow into a fetus*
- *Prepares the breast tissue to secrete milk*

Progesterone dominates the last two weeks of a woman's cycle, dampening her sex drive. On the plus side, it's a natural sedative, making her chill and feel mellow—at least until she gets PMS in the last few days of her cycle.

## DO MEN PRODUCE ESTROGEN AND PROGESTERONE?

Absolutely. Just as women have their inner-T male, you have your inner female. Your testes create most of your T, E and progesterone; your adrenals and pituitary glands also generate small amounts of progesterone.

---

**NOTE**» YOUNG MEN HAVE A
T:E RATIO OF 50:1.

---

Although the Big T rules, you literally wouldn't be a man without estrogen and progesterone. For starters, progesterone is the key ingredient in making your testosterone. E helps to grow your penis and testicles and to create your sperm. What's more, E helps develop manly muscles and stimulates the growth of beards and body hair. Strong bone density, a healthy heart, good brain function and memory also depend on having the right T:progesterone ratio.

Sex hormones are always performing a balancing act. It can get pretty dramatic when they go out of kilter, which you may have observed on a monthly basis when your lover is PMS and maybe not so loving. Guys don't have cyclical hormone changes; their imbalance happens gradually over time until it reaches a point where it can cause troubling symptoms.

---

**NOTE**» AFTER AGE THIRTY, T LEVELS
DECREASE STEADILY BY 1%-2% A YEAR.

---

So that means that by the time you're fifty-five, you have 25% to 50% less T, which alters its ratio to E and progesterone. Does that make a major difference in your mate's and your life? Actually, it's so considerable that we've devoted an entire chapter to it. In *Andropause: Men's Climate Change,* you'll be briefed on men's weather from the age of 50 on and get the forecast for your potency, sex life, appearance, health and the new ways you might look at things.

## *YOUR LOVER'S MONTHLY FORECAST*

It took us a while to get here, but we are about to embark on the super practical, vitally important briefing on how your partner's menstrual cycle affects her weather. If you're like most men, you're probably clueless about the huge hormonal shifts she goes through every month. It probably never even occurred to you to talk to her about it. Since women have been having these ups and downs for million of years, the question is "why aren't men interested?"

For starters, guys can't relate to a female's cycle because they don't have any personal experience to compare it to: it's not remotely similar to how their own bodies work. Then there's a kind of "messy" taboo to it, and a history of religions considering women dirty when they have their periods. Plus females aren't particularly eager to discuss it either.

Bottom line is that men don't see the upside to understanding it. But, we're here to tell you that your lover's

75

fluctuating hormones can have an enormous influence on her emotions and behavior, ergo, you and your quality of life. It is your business. And you're a guy; you like to know how to fix things. You might finally get the information that won't leave you helpless as her weather changes.

## WHAT IF MY LOVER IS PAST HAVING A CYCLE?

We talk about peri and postmenopause in our *Women's Climate Change* chapter, but we recommend getting an understanding of the menstrual cycle anyway because it:

- *Clarifies what was going on with your mate in the past*
- *Gives you a better grasp of her menopausal symptoms and problems*
- *Helps you comprehend other females in your personal and professional life who still get their periods*

## THE MENSTRUAL CYCLE

Estrogen is named for the estrus cycle, which is when a woman is hottest and most receptive to mating. In fact, estrogen and testosterone are at their height and her libido is in full throttle when she's ovulating. That's how Nature makes sure there are babies.

A woman's menstrual cycle is all about her body preparing an egg to get fertilized and the adjustments it makes when that doesn't happen. Her cycle starts on the first day she starts bleeding and goes until the first day of her next period, when she starts bleeding again. It usually lasts 24-28 days. All women are different, so your lover's reactions will vary, but here is a general look at what's going on physically, emotionally and psychologically during her "monthlies." Having this information helps you predict your lover's weather and gives you some practical navigational tools that make for smoother flights.

---

**NOTE**» *THE RULE OF THUMB IS, THE MORE E, THE BETTER SHE CAN FEEL AND LOOK. THE MORE IMBALANCED HER HORMONES, THE WORSE SHE CAN FEEL.*

---

Women, don't be surprised if you find you weren't completely tuned into your own cycle and have some insights of your own.

## WEEK ONE: MENSTRUATION

Day 1: She bleeds. Progesterone prepared her inner lining to hold her fertilized egg. When that doesn't happen, the lining is discharged along with some blood and other products.

That's when your lover's cycle begins and you start counting.

Her bleeding starts moderately, increases, and then slowly tapers off. Some women usually have a light blood flow, others a medium or a heavy flow. Since most women's periods last four to eight days, the specific amount of time your woman menstruates probably falls within that range, but can change over the course of her life.

During this phase, especially the first few days, your mate might need personal time and space to go within and take care of herself. Encourage her to do it.

## IS THIS THE RIGHT TIME TO BE ROMANTIC?

It depends on how your lover feels. Some women get cramps, have a lot of menstrual or abdominal pain, headaches, feel bloated or get depressed. This is obviously a "no."

Others just think it is messy and would rather not. That is a maybe. Maybe you can turn her on. Maybe she can wear a tampon and you can give each other oral sex. Try at least for the oral sex.

Some women are pain free and are not fussy about blood. Their estrogen and testosterone levels are beginning to rise and they're feeling positive, energized and sexual. Get a plastic sheet or a towel and you're good to go.

## WEEK TWO: BLUE SKIES

Estrogen rules and testosterone is its libidinous partner. Your lover is at her physical best. Her energy is high, she feels more confident, attractive and sexy. She spreads her wings, takes off and heads for the mile high club. These are the most favorable flight conditions.

Your woman is more verbal and her long-term memory is sharpest now. So maybe she'll remember even MORE things you did or said that you cannot recall. But since she's in a sexy, positive frame of mind, she's biologically in the mood to make love, not war.

This is the go-for-it week. Make mad, passionate love. Take the time, don't miss out. Kiss. Suck. Intercourse. Oral. Anal. Whatever gives you both pleasure. It's a good week for a romantic vacation.

---

*CAUTION» SEXUAL ENERGY BUILDS UP QUICKLY FOR WOMEN DURING THIS TIME. THEY CAN BECOME TUMESCENT (TOO MUCH SEXUAL ENERGY). IF THEY DON'T GET SEXUAL RELIEF, THEY CAN GET DIFFICULT.*

---

Somewhere in this week, or a little later, she ovulates; her body is at its peak of readiness for reproduction, and her libido crescendos. Live for today, because tomorrow, her libido lessens.

## OVULATION

Ignore this at your peril. Ovulation generally occurs 14-16 days before women have their periods. So, if your woman is fairly regular at 28 days, you subtract: 28-14 =14 days; 28-16= 12 days. So she is ovulating somewhere between the 12th and 14th day of her cycle.

## HOW CAN YOU TELL IF/WHEN YOUR LOVER IS OVULATING?

Learning when your mate ovulates is an excellent thing to do as a couple. It creates intimacy and trust as well as safety. This is how to do it:

Get a basal thermometer and have her take her temperature first thing every morning when she wakes up. When it spikes, she's ovulating.

Watch her discharge. When it's thick and tacky and it forms a solid string, between her thumb and forefingers, she's ovulating.

See what day in her cycle these two events occur and diligently keep a diary.

Keep a diary for a long enough period of time to see if your lover is regular and what her pattern is. If she has an irregular cycle, you have to be very diligent with birth control if you don't want kids, or very amorous if you do. Ditto if her pattern changes, which can be due to stress, environmental factors, illness etc.

## DOES MY LOVER ONLY GET PREGNANT ON THE DAY SHE OVULATES?

No!

---

**WARNING**» A WOMAN CAN GET PREGNANT
FROM INTERCOURSE BEFORE AND
AFTER SHE OVULATES.

---

A woman can only conceive after she ovulates. Although her egg just lives for 24 hours, your eager sperm lives for 3-4 days, and in some cases 6-7 days. If you've had intercourse before your lover ovulates, your sperm can already be inside her, ready and waiting for that egg so it can make babies. The same is true if you had sex during the 24 hours after she ovulated: egg + sperm = you're a dad.

## WEEK THREE: HER LAID BACK WEEK

Yesterday she was hot, but today she's not. What happened? After ovulation, your partner's libido is dampened by progesterone levels that rise to up to 140 times higher than her estrogen levels. The ever-efficient progesterone also neutralizes her testosterone.

Men, lower your expectations. Don't anticipate the hot sex of the previous week, but you can still have great sex. Connecting to your partner emotionally and spiritually is sex at its deepest and doesn't require high estrogen and testosterone levels.

While your lover's sex drive has decreased, she is feeling mellower. Progesterone, also known as "Mother Nature's Prozac for Girls," lowers her anxiety, lessens her anger and stabilizes her mood, which is great news for peace of mind and for your relationship.

Since progesterone makes your woman thirstier, hungrier, and heightens her taste buds, this is also a fine time to make food play a bigger role in your sensual life.

Sedated by her progesterone, your mate tends to feel tired, sleepy and fuzzy-brained. Encourage your baby to get her beauty rest and don't suggest projects that require high energy.

---

**NOTE**» *PROGESTERONE CAUSES BREAST TENDERNESS. ASK YOUR LOVER ABOUT THAT AND ADJUST ACCORDINGLY.*

---

## WEEK FOUR: STORMY WEATHER

**Q: What's the difference between a PMS woman and a terrorist?**

**A: You can negotiate with a terrorist.**

This is the week of the dreaded PMS—*Premenstrual symptoms,* or more descriptively, Pissy Mood Syndrome, Pardon My Sobbing, and Pack My Stuff. It is now that the lovely Ms. Jekyll can relinquish command to the dangerous Ms. Hyde.

## WHAT IS PMS?

Progesterone withdraws two to three days before your woman's period. Even though there might not be much estrogen, if its level is high in relation to progesterone, your lady gets hormonally unbalanced. Fasten your seatbelt and be

82

prepared for a bumpy ride. As many as 90% of women have crappy symptoms before they get their periods.

Physically, your partner can feel anything from the rare, "just fine" to moderate to strong reactions. She can feel bloated and have intensely uncomfortable sensations: cramps, abdominal pain, migraines and breast discomfort caused by premenstrual water retention.

She may get depressed, moody, cry easily, start a fight, and become antagonistic or prickly. She can get very critical and negative about herself, you and your relationship. Reminding her how she was really happy with things last week may not work; her lowered estrogen levels aren't there to support analytical thinking.

---

*CAUTION» DO NOT DO OR SAY ANYTHING THAT COULD BE REMOTELY INTERPRETED AS CRITICAL DURING THIS PMS TIME.*

---

Subjects such as her appearance, weight or attractiveness are hurricane country and strictly off-limits. Save any problems or relationship issues for later. No matter what you say, she may hear it as negative.

Encourage her to take care of herself. Support her exercising, meditating or praying, taking her vitamins and minerals—especially calcium, magnesium and vitamin B6.

## FINDING OUT ABOUT YOUR LOVER'S CYCLE

Now you can add your partner's menstrual cycle to other fascinating sex topics, like STDs and contraceptives. Communication is the key. Read this together and let her tell you what happens to her during her cycle. It's a great team building exercise. Her keeping a diary of her reactions would be immensely beneficial for both of you. That way you'll both become pretty good weather forecasters.

In every flight manual there is a performance section that is full of charts and graphs about how the aircraft will perform in any given circumstance. Here is a chart that will help you have at least an inkling of how your lover might act in some given circumstances.

---

**NOTE**» THE DATES IN THE MENSTRUAL
CYCLE CHART ARE ONLY APPROXIMATIONS.
EVERY WOMAN'S DATES WILL VARY EVEN
FROM MONTH TO MONTH DEPENDING ON THE
CIRCUMSTANCES OF HER LIFE.

---

## THE MENSTRUAL CYCLE CHART

| Days | Physical | Emotional | Hormonal |
|---|---|---|---|
| 1 – 8 | Bleeding starts—varying discomfort. Bleeding ends between days 4 & 8 | Needs quiet time. May not feel like having sex | Hormone production minimal |
| 6 - 16 | Stronger, more alert, physically adept, verbal | Confident, sexy, up-beat, feels more attractive | Testosterone and estrogen production high |
| 14 - 16 | Temperature spikes discharge sticky Egg descends and is ready for conception | Ready for sex, needs sexual release | Testosterone peaks |
| 16 - 21 | Thirsty, hungry, fuzzy thinking, low energy | Mellow, can be seduced | Progesterone spikes and testosterone and estrogen drop |
| 21 - 28 | Can feel bloated, cramping | May feel irritable, depressed, argumentative | Progesterone falls off |

Here is another chart to help clarify atmospheric conditions. It compares estrogen with testosterone, so you can easily see the differences.

## THE TESTOSTERONE VS. ESTROGEN COMPARISON CHART

| TESTOSTERONE | ESTROGEN |
|---|---|
| *BIOLOGY* | *BIOLOGY* |
| Floods brain in womb making male brain | Floods brain in the womb making female brain |
| Forms the male sex organs | Forms the female sex organs |
| Surges in puberty | Surges in puberty |
| Creates the male secondary sex characteristics | Creates female secondary sex characteristics |
| Responsible for erections | Regulates the menstrual cycle |
| Contributes to frequency and duration of erections | Dominates the first 2 weeks of cycle |
| | Prepares uterus for pregnancy |
| | Dramatically decreases in menopause |
| | Small amounts in men |
| Men have 10-100xs more circulating in their blood stream | Increases as men age |

| TESTOSTERONE | ESTROGEN |
|---|---|
| *HEALTH* | *HEALTH* |
| Maintains strength | Maintains good brain function |
| Maintains mental and physical energy | Protects the heart |
| Maintains bone density | Maintains bone density |
| *IN SEX* | *IN SEX* |
| Responsible for sex drive | Responsible for fertility |
| Released into men's blood stream every 17-60 seconds | Lubricates the vagina |
| Makes men think about sex | Heightens sensitivity and pleasure |
| In men, highest levels in the morning | Boosts libido |
| Drive for casual sex with many partners | Increases the strength of orgasm |
| Don't need foreplay | Peaks during ovulation |
| T surge after orgasm blocks oxytocin | Produces sperm in men |
| *EMOTION* | *EMOTION* |
| Prenatal T blocks growth of emotion centers in the brain | Prenatal E grows emotional brain centers |
| Steady T drip stabilizes emotions | Hormonal cycle affects emotions |
| Less emotional | More emotional |

| TESTOSTERONE | ESTROGEN |
|---|---|
| ***SPEECH*** | ***SPEECH*** |
| Prenatal T blocks language centers in the brain | Prenatal E grows the language centers in the brain |
| Less verbal | More verbal |
| Action-oriented | Highest verbal tendency in 2nd week of cycle |
| ***OBSERVATIONAL SKILLS*** | ***OBSERVATIONAL SKILLS*** |
| Prenatal T blocks the growth of brain observation centers | Prenatal E grows the observational centers in the brain |
| Less observant | More observant |
| | Most observant in 2nd week of cycle |
| ***MEMORY*** | ***MEMORY*** |
| Less emotional memory | Better emotional memory |
| | Best emotional memory in 2nd week of cycle |

# THE PROGESTERONE CHART

| PROGESTERONE CHART |
| :---: |
| **BIOLOGY** |
| Regulates menstrual cycle |
| Dominates the third week of cycle |
| Makes a cushion for fertilized egg to grow in |
| Helps sustain pregnancy |
| Small amounts in men |
| Contributes to frequency and duration of erections |
| In men, decreases in ratio to E as they age |
| Dramatically decreases in menopause |
| **IN SEX** |
| Dampens sex drive in women |
| Produces testosterone in men |
| **EMOTION** |
| Natural sedative in women |

## THE ESTROGEN QUIZ

**Rate your answers on the following scale:**

Almost Never = 1

Rarely = 2

Sometimes = 3

Often = 4

Almost Always =5

1. I have a deep emotional life. _____

2. I have many moods. _____

3. I'm tuned into and curious about other people's emotions. _____

4. I'm good at reading people's emotions by the expressions on their faces or from the tones of their voices. _____

5. My emotions play a big part in helping me to set goals and make decisions. _____

6. I love talking. _____

7. I prefer a layered, association of ideas to concise communication. _____

8. I can usually recall what my partner and I said and did, especially if the situation was emotionally charged. _____

9. I enjoy character-driven books, TV and movies more than action-driven ones. _____

10. I have glossy hair and moist skin. _____

**TOTAL** ____

**If you scored:**

40-50, you are very influenced by estrogen.

10-20, you are minimally influenced by estrogen.

21-39, you are in the middle range.

## WHAT'S ON THE RADAR?

You might have had an inkling about how estrogen affects your partner, but there's a good chance you don't know about oxytocin, her other super-fuel. It can be quite a revelation to see how this love and bonding hormone makes her thoughts and actions so different from yours. Here we go.

# CHAPTER THREE

*II Oxytocin makes the weather warm and balmy, and can boost it to hot and steamy. Fighter pilots and lovers like this kind of weather and both acclimate quickly. II*

## *OXYTOCIN: LOVE IN THE SUN*

Do you know how your partner:

- Smiles and coos over babies, puppies, kittens and even you?

- Wants to hug and cuddle far more than you do?

- Wants lots of foreplay when you'd prefer to penetrate her immediately?

- Wants to linger in bed and continue to bond after sex, when you just want to go to sleep or move on to your next activity?

Those are samples of oxytocin (OT) in action. It's aptly nicknamed the "love hormone," "bonding hormone," "cuddle hormone," and "the maternal hormone." Actually, OT does double-duty, acting as a hormone when it circulates in our blood, and as a brain chemical when it carries messages in our brain and nervous systems. Together, they motivate bonding and produce powerful and satisfying feelings of love, affection and closeness.

---

**NOTE**» *ESTROGEN MAGNIFIES OXYTOCIN AND WOMEN HAVE 10 TIMES MORE THAN MEN DO.*

---

These are no mere, ordinary facts. They are sun-through-the-clouds facts that illuminate fundamental causes of so many of your lover's most passionate needs, drives and behaviors.

---

**NOTE**» *OT "TURNS ON" IN RESPONSE TO THE RIGHT STIMULI, LIKE BONDING, THEN FADES. THE WRONG STIMULI, LIKE STRESS AND NOT FEELING SAFE, EITHER BLOCK IT OR TURN IT OFF.*

---

## THE MATERNAL HORMONE

Women are built for love, engineered to bond because they are made to be mothers. Oxytocin comes from the Greek for "swift birth." That's makes sense because it makes the cervix dilate prior to birth and causes the contractions that push the baby out into the world. This huge surge of oxytocin (300 times more than normal) inundates the mother's brain and body after natural birth and creates profound love and a deep, lasting tie with her newborn.

And then, as her baby sucks her nipples, oxytocin is stimulated, making her milk flow and engendering more loving, nurturing and bonding feelings.

Why is this so important? Because while estrogen prepares a woman to become pregnant and gives her the tools to understand her baby's needs, it doesn't create a reason to stick around, raise and protect it. Oxytocin does. Looking into her child's eyes, smelling its delicious scent, touching it, kissing it and communicating to it all trigger OT and strengthen the love and commitment to her child.

Your mate is super-sensitive to these physical cues, but her natural OT high can be easily activated, child or no child, in her everyday life. And Nature made triply sure she wants it to be by rewarding her with even more good feelings.

---

***NOTE***» *WHEN OXYTOCIN SURGES, IT ACTIVATES THE RELEASE OF SEROTONIN AND DOPAMINE.*

---

Just to remind you, serotonin promotes feelings of well-being and reduces anxiety. *Dopamine* is associated with euphoria, pleasure, and addiction—the drive to keep repeating whatever caused those oh-so-good feelings. This oxytocin/ serotonin/dopamine rush is a powerful incentive

95

for connecting—one your mate wants to get on a stable, ongoing basis. How does she do it? By developing relationships with kids, mates, families, friends and communities.

## BONDING

Nature doesn't casually dispense qualities. A female isn't endowed with the muscular strength of a man and can't physically ward off predators, invaders or hostile men. Historically, she and her children survived because she created intimate connections and allies who wanted to protect her and her children. Your modern woman may be educated, independent and financially self-sufficient, but relationships are probably still her instinctively dominant priority.

Therefore, oxytocin both impels your mate to connect and rewards her practically and emotionally for doing so. Bonding gives her immense pleasure, shapes her interactions and is a big measure of her success in life. When it comes to your relationship, intimate, heartfelt interactions make your woman want you more than anything else does. When she asks for romance, what she is really asking for is that you do things that allow her to open, feel close to you and experience the love. She wants a healthy committed relationship because it gives her a safe space to be vulnerable and create the love.

Sounds simple enough, but it may not be an easy task for you to execute, due to the oft-repeated fact that your T blocks oxytocin.

Yes, in one of those baffling contradictions, Nature created a male machine that counters intimacy and relationship. Uh oh. Guess it didn't want its "providers and protectors" to feel too connected to the animals they had to kill or the enemies they had to fight. You might be familiar with the T vs. OT fallout: misunderstandings and conflicts. It's not a total mismatch, however, because men also have oxytocin.

## OXYTOCIN AND MEN

To get a tangible idea of how oxytocin affects your partner and why bonding is so valuable to her, think about your own sexual experience. Although your oxytocin levels can be as much as ten times lower than hers, it still works its magic on you. You release OT, and consequently dopamine and serotonin, when you're kissing, touching and getting aroused during sex, and especially when you orgasm.

The oxytocin receptors in your penis cause the contractions that make you ejaculate. At the moment of climax, your OT levels shoot up to match what your woman may naturally experience a few times a day. It's your highest levels and the biggest bonding experience you get.

When you're ecstatic you can feel an incredible loving connection to your partner. You might even say: "I love you." Hopefully, you still like her later.

Not only is OT responsible for your contractions, it also deepens the feelings from fondling and kissing that stimulates, strengthens and prolongs your erection.

Don't underestimate the power of an oxytocin high. Our greatest sexual experiences are when we "disappear" and merge with our partner. That feeling of "oneness" is what people describe as spiritual or religious. And it's an important emotional reason why men keep asking for more.

There's a lot of truth in the saying: "If the sex is good, he'll want the relationship. If the relationship is good, she'll want the sex." When you make love with your wife or partner, repeated connection fosters ongoing caring, and devotion. The repeated intimacy is more than emotional or spiritual: as the dedicated pathways in your brain for having sex and bonding with your one special woman get stronger, so does your willingness to commit to her.

Remember that, ladies. Also, it's a good idea to touch your man frequently to engender those bonding feelings in him.

---

*NOTE» GUYS NEED TO BE TOUCHED 2-3 TIMES MORE OFTEN THAN FEMALES TO SUSTAIN THE SAME OT LEVELS FEMALES ENJOY.*

---

Of course sex isn't the only time men experience oxytocin or connection. Kids, pets, families, buddies, etc. can evoke those warm and gratifying feelings of attachment.

---

**NOTE**» *AS IN ALL HORMONES, THERE'S A RANGE OF OT IN MEN, MAKING THEM MORE OR LESS LIKELY TO EXHIBIT OT'S CHARACTERISTICS.*

---

Since testosterone blocks oxytocin, guys are more susceptible to the gentling effects of OT when their T levels go down. When does that happen? When they marry or have a committed relationship and when their child is born and they hold it. The other biggie, and one you're destined to experience, is andropause.

As men age, their T declines by 1%-2% a year. At the same time, their E rises. By the time they reach their late 50s most men have more E than their menopausal partners. Both hormonal conditions make men more susceptible to oxytocin's effects. In this new climate, you could find yourself discovering strange and wondrous things, like the joy of cuddling and increasing compassion. Our *Andropause: Men's Climate Change* chapter tells you all about what to expect.

## THE HIGH–T WOMAN

With the exception of andropause, a female with high testosterone can have similar emotional, psychological and sexual reactions as men. So if your partner is a goddess of the high testosterone persuasion, there are many areas where she'll see things the way males do. Keep that in mind as you read on through oxytocin's impact on women, starting with sex.

## HOT AND STEAMY

### Q: Why do women fake orgasm?
### A: Because men fake foreplay.

It's true. Skip foreplay and there's a good chance she won't be turned on enough to climax. So, if you're ever tempted to omit it, burn the following into your memory disc: OT makes your lover a sensual creature; she's much more sensitive to sight, sound, taste, touch and odors than you are. Therefore, her response to music, candles, incense and good food prior to sex is greater than yours. A light stroke that you might not even feel can send shivers of pleasure all through her body.

But your touch does more than just turn her on: the oxytocin it releases in her brain makes her feel calm, tender and trusting. Everything in the sexual act—from eye-gazing, cuddling, kissing and sucking on her nipples to stimulating her vagina and cervix—releases oxytocin. It surges through her when she orgasms and afterwards makes her face and chest flush.

So, if you want great sex, spend the time stroking, kissing, licking and sucking. The more you do, the more connected and excited she'll get. That will make you both happy.

This might also be the time to keep in mind this vital fact:

---

**WARNING**» *STRESS BLOCKS OXYTOCIN*
*IN MEN AND WOMEN.*

---

Therefore, erotic bliss depends on having a conflict-free, safe environment that enables her to be vulnerable and allow her OT to flow.

## WHY DOES SHE WANT TO LINGER AFTER SEX?

*To him: he's done, on to something else.*

*To her: it's cuddle time!*

After orgasm, oxytocin floods your lover's system and estrogen boosts its effects. She's like a kitten that wants to snuggle up to you and purr for a long time, and maybe do it all over again.

You, on the other hand, are ready for the next event. After your fantastic burst of oxytocin, at climax, your testosterone quickly builds and brings your oxytocin levels back to normal. Cuddling is not on your agenda.

This is tricky, so handle with care. Men and women are in two totally different spaces. To get the idea of where your lover is, consider your sexual fantasies and your drive for hotter, better, higher sex. She probably has those desires too, but now she could be in a sort of post-coital female dream.

Blissed-out and getting more blissed-out by the minute, she wants the intimacy and caring to grow and to be even closer. If she loves you, she wants love to soar. And of course, she wants you to feel the same way. That could be a scary thought when you're not feeling anything remotely similar.

What you don't want to do is abruptly withdraw because her high OT energy makes her extremely sensitive. If you do, your lover will feel cut off, disappointed and hurt. She might cynically conclude that "you just wanted sex" and now that it's over you don't care about her anymore. Ever heard that?

---

**WARNING**» *YOU NEVER WANT HER TO GO TO THAT "ONLY FOR SEX" DEFAULT. COMMITTED OR SINGLE, IT'S TOXIC FOR YOUR SEX LIFE.*

---

Making a smooth transition is the best policy. Definitely discuss your opposing needs and compromise. We find fifteen minutes of snuggling before going off to the next activity usually works for both parties.

---

**NOTE**» *LADIES, HIS NOT HAVING THE SAME EXPERIENCE DOESN'T MEAN THAT HE CARES ANY LESS.*

---

## DATING IN THE SUN

There's a whole series of gender conflicts that can result from our differing "after glows," short and long-range.

There's also an etiquette that you can learn and do that will make your dating life sunnier. For starters, acknowledge your lover after sex.

---

**CAUTION**» NO 'WHAM, BAM,
THANK YOU MA'AM'.

---

She needs to know that you appreciate her opening to you. Do so before you get out of bed and then again the next day. It's rude and ungentlemanly to take her for granted.

And there's a price each of you will pay if you do!

Females tend to be sensitive. Not communicating the following day can lead to her feeling discarded and concluding you just want to talk to her when "you want sex." There it is again, the deadly default.

The emotions she could feel, particularly if you just started getting intimate are not pretty: anger, resentment, low self-esteem, humiliation, and shame to name a few.

The longer you wait, the worse it can get. Probably the only scenario she won't envision is the real one: you like her, are into your work and looking forward to seeing her again.

---

**NOTE**» LADIES, TALK TO YOUR MAN ABOUT
YOUR NEED FOR ACKNOWLEDGMENT.

---

It's hard to believe, women, but he's probably clueless and will be grateful for some concrete way to make you happy.

Oblivious husbands will also welcome the information for the same reason.

## WHY DON'T WOMEN WANT TO HAVE SEX RIGHT AWAY?

After the sexual revolution, men got lucky. Very lucky. And maybe spoilt. With increased numbers of sexually liberated women wanting to jump into bed after a date or two, guys might feel entitled to sex. However, there are many equally sexually liberated women who want to wait.

Why? Aside from not knowing you, not wanting casual sex and potential STDS, etc. they also may have learnt that having sex right away doesn't work for them. While your T shouts: "Have sex with as many women as you can," their E and OT cautions: "Look for someone who will stay around." Especially if they have been hurt.

## TRUST

Trust is the glue that holds relationships and society together. When we trust someone, we are open and vulnerable to being affected by him or her. We're also more empathetic, caring, giving and cooperative. Oxytocin and trust are intimately connected because OT surges both when we're being trusted and when we trust another. It's very painful if we're betrayed or misled.

---

**NOTE**» *EVEN A 20 SECOND HUG TRIGGERS*
*THE TRUST CIRCUITS IN A WOMAN'S BRAIN.*

---

A high E, high OT woman could bond very strongly after sex and start caring deeply for her partner. She can't just turn her emotions off so it's painful for her when guys don't feel the same way. This can apply to everything from one-night stands to longer relationships.

Hopefully, you adhere to the Code of Honor and don't mislead women. If you're just interested in getting laid and your date thinks you're interested in HER, she could suffer when you jump out of bed or break up. So, while you may never think about some woman you've spent one or a few nights with again, she could be wounded for months. This might be hard for you to understand since you probably don't have many dark emotional repercussions after casual sex. So let us explain:

For thousands of years, women having sex outside of marriage were considered sluts. Although you don't see your date that way, she might feel dirty if you disappear after having sex with her. Old lies die hard. We've seen many a lovely, accomplished woman who felt rejected, humiliated and shamed after a one-night stand. Numerous others have confessed to feeling degraded and having low self-esteem after giving into pressure to have sex they weren't ready for and didn't really want. These negative thoughts and emotions bury into her subconscious and can be triggered if you treat her in a careless way. Don't. Be a trustable man.

## WHAT IF I DO JUST WANT TO GET LAID?

There's nothing wrong with recreational sex as long as you and your date are on the same page. Do you want a one-night stand, friends with benefits, a mostly sexual connection? If that's what she's looking for, you scored. If not, no sex. So what? Find someone with similar needs. The point is, be crystal clear about what you're doing. Then let the fun begin.

What if you both agree to just have sex and she gets attached, but wants to continue? She's an adult; if that's what she wants, why say "no"? Because it's only a convenient justification to get what you want. It's hurting her now and will hurt her more in the inevitable end. It's a Code of Honor moment: "Do no harm." Let her go.

## WHAT IF I REALLY DO WANT A RELATIONSHIP?

Few of us escape painful breakups, so we tend to be more discerning as we get older and wiser. A woman who's been hurt wants to protect her heart. Having learned how attached she can become when she has sex, she needs more time to be sure that you are not Mr. Wrong.

Then of course, she might be looking for a husband or a committed partner and doesn't want to waste her time with someone who doesn't fit the bill.

If you want what she wants, give her whatever time she needs to get to know and trust you. Communicate. Talk about your sexual needs and ask her what her time frame is for having sex. It's not a question of right or wrong: she requires what she requires and you require what you require. If what she says works for you, continue courting, build your connection and make mad, passionate love when the time is right.

## WHY DO MEN PUT OFF COMMITTED RELATIONSHIPS?

Typically, the man is the one who's reluctant to commit and his girlfriend is the one to ask: "Where is this relationship going?" Which translated means, "when are we going to commit/get married?" Her E & OT make her ready for takeoff, while his T still has him doing his preflight inspection.

Even if the sex is good and the man adores his lover, he might still be reluctant to take the plunge. Guys are programmed "to inseminate every woman they can" and it can be tough to hit "delete."

Many panicked men have sat in our office, afraid to make the wrong decision: "I can't imagine having sex with just one woman for the rest of my life"; "I don't know if I can be faithful"; and "It feels like prison" are examples of their dread. On the other hand, they're afraid to lose their partner, who is arguably the best thing that ever happened to them.

To these torn men we quote the reassuring fact: married couples have more and better sex than singles. They are also healthier and live longer.

---

**NOTE**» *OF COURSE, CRASHING AND BURNING IN OTHER RELATIONSHIPS, A MESSY DIVORCE, ALIMONY AND CHILDCARE CAN MAKE A GUY COMMITMENT-PHOBIC.*

---

## CONFLICTING WEATHER PATTERNS

It's really amazing how opposed testosterone and oxytocin are. Nature clearly intended to differentiate the emotional, psychological and social reactions of males and females for survival of the species. The question is, did Nature think through its design for survival of relationships? Maybe Nature had more on its cosmic mind than to worry about the finer points of gender harmony. That's for us to work out, apparently. Confusions and questions abound. Here are some answers.

## WHY DOES SHE WANT TO BE TOGETHER SO MUCH?

Your partner's desire for togetherness is simply a manifestation of her drive for relationship and bonding. It's like her wanting to be close after sex. Connection turns your partner's OT faucet on, and she doesn't want to turn it off. It's the pleasure principle: if you're spending time together and enjoying each other, why not spend more time and enjoy each other more?

What she doesn't understand is that, although you also appreciate feeling close, you can only get so close for so long. Where her biology dictates intimacy, yours dictates space. Her expectations for connection can make you feel stressed out and smothered.

---

*NOTE» MEN'S CORTISOL (STRESS) CAN RISE WHEN THEY REACH THEIR LIMIT FOR CONNECTION OR COMMUNICATION.*

---

Men often have to go into their "caves" for hours or days in order to get in touch with themselves. After they've regrouped, they're ready and eager to make another foray into togetherness.

It's important to talk over and resolve this disparity of needs with your mate. Let her know that you love her, but that you have to take care of yourself so that you can take care of her. It helps to give her some idea of how long you'll be so she can adjust her anticipation. Not that explaining this necessarily solves everything. She might still feel lonely or disappointed, but at least she'll understand you have different needs and won't feel abandoned. It also sets the stage for the two cure-alls for relationship success: negotiation and  compromise.

## WHY DOES SHE GET ANGRY WHEN I WORK LONG HOURS?

*To him: working late or on weekends is required to succeed and provide.*

*To her: it means he's neglecting her and the kids and has lousy values.*

**||** *It's true that men's theatre of operations tends to be their careers. Like their ancestors whose success was measured by their hunting prowess, males often define themselves by what they achieve outside of their homes. They usually focus on a personal mission that tests their abilities, reveals their potential and gives them a sense of personal power. Flying fighters was my testing ground. I didn't think twice about risking my life and being away from my family if I could be the best pilot I could be. Like a lot of men, it didn't occur to me to do the work it would take to make my love and family life stellar.* **//**

Women are inclined by their oxytocin to have a different take on their careers. Even though they might be equally ambitious and successful in their careers, intimacy with their partners, friends, or family remains a priority.

There are more female than male college graduates in the U.S. and most women work. But, business models are male, hierarchal and competitive and our culture stresses economic success. As a result, we see a lot more female clients, especially young women, who are measuring their self-esteem by career success. Nevertheless, they're still intent on finding the right man. And working moms are still deeply attached to their kids and committed to giving them the time and attention they need to thrive, and they expect you to do your part.

It's a fact that working long hours is a requisite to success in many careers. It could be easier for you than for your mate because the system is aligned with your biology and your sense of purpose. She, however, can find it separates her from her feminine core and drains her. Conversely, creating healthy relationships reconnects her to her femininity, satisfies her emotionally, and gives her a sense of self-worth.

The weather gets particularly stormy when a man neglects a stay-at-home mom. While some job-obsessed fathers may make time for their kids, not giving their mate the time, attention and communication they crave sets the stage for a cold-front with thunderstorms in its wake.

It's frustrating to be criticized for working hard to better yourself and provide economically. It's also depressing for your mate to feel your work takes precedence over her. So what do you do? We can tell you two things not to do:

- *Do not be a workaholic.*

- *Do not make her feel unimportant.*

These are formulas for disaster that result in your mate becoming increasingly hostile. The upshot is that your work becomes her enemy; she doesn't support your doing it and may even say or do things to undermine it. And surprise, she doesn't want to have sex with you. Eventually she might just give up and say goodbye to the relationship altogether.

So, the real questions become: How much time are you spending with your family? Is there a realistic balance between your work and your relationship? Are you absent because your job genuinely requires it, like a physician on call? Are you more focused on pleasing your clients and managers than your partner? Are you so passionate about your work that you exclude less interesting pursuits, like bonding with her or your kids? Or are you so consumed with your ambition that you don't appreciate spending time with them?

Relationships don't create themselves, so if you're absent and want one, you're going to have to work hard to change your value system and break old, ingrained habits. Whatever the cause, it's back to the negotiating table and finding practical compromises with your mate. For starters, you can set aside quality time when you get home. Giving each other a hello kiss, and then spending even 20 to 30 minutes communicating can create a good connection. We like to have dinner together and go over our day. As a couple you need to agree on job boundaries and when to say "yes" or "no" to working late or on weekends. On the proactive, fun side, make plans for date nights, weekends and vacations. And hallelujah, you might even have that amazing, healing OT-releasing sex that makes both of you happy, loving, cooperative, and generous.

Now on to the next weather watch, the T vs. OT differences in communication.

## WHY DOES SHE TALK SO MUCH?

*To him: she talks endlessly.*

*To her: men are communicatively impaired.*

Estrogen isn't the only reason women are champion talkers. Oxytocin is a major contributor because speaking gets them, but not men, high from the pleasurable OT/serotonin/dopamine rush. At times your lover can get so much joy from talking that only having an orgasm gives her a bigger hit. Needless to say you'd never stop talking if you were affected that way.

Which is why your partner may take it personally if you're not as chatty as she is. Talking to her girlfriends creates intimacy and the kind of ecstasy that she wants to experience with you. She doesn't understand that you're not having a similar reaction, and therefore assumes that you don't want to share and get closer with her. You, on the other hand, don't understand what she's carrying on about; as far as you're concerned, you've said everything you need to say.

---

***CAUTION***» *YOUR WOMAN CAN FEEL LONELY AND FRUSTRATED IF SHE'S NOT GETTING THE COMMUNICATION SHE NEEDS.*

---

A lonely woman is not a happy woman, which guarantees you won't be happy either. Since brains are plastic, behavior can be altered. You need to go beyond your comfort zone and improve your verbal and listening skills. In turn, your lover needs to stretch by being more tolerant when you're not as communicative as she is.

## LISTENING

Good communication consists of people expressing themselves and being heard and understood. Have you ever witnessed two females locked in a seamless conversation mind-meld? Their intoxicating OT cocktail flows along with their dialogue, getting them higher and higher. Maybe you don't have the innate machinery to reach those lofty heights, but you can practice and improve.

Here are some tips:

The more your mate communicates, the better she feels. Therefore if she has something to say, let her say it—all of it.

*CAUTION*» *DON'T INTERRUPT A WOMAN'S FLOW OF CONVERSATION. IF YOU DO, SHE CAN FEEL HURT AND ALIENATED, WHICH NEGATES THE WHOLE PURPOSE OF THE EXERCISE.*

This is particularly true if she was telling you anything emotional, important to her, or about a problem. In those cases, you want her to talk to get it all out. Just keep repeating these three magic words: "Is there more?" until she's done. Then watch the sun come out, along with affection and a better relationship—sort of like when she climaxes.

It may seem like a torturous task at first, but you want her to be happy, don't you? And along with love, bonding and a better relationship, you'll have better sex.

Communication definitely belongs in your seduction/foreplay toolkit. Anything that turns your lover's OT on can get her in the mood for making love. Being good at chatting up women is what makes those silver-tongued pick-up artists so successful. Special tricks or rehearsed banter isn't required, as some dating books would have you believe. Women find men who can talk and listen to them sexy and as the conversation flows, increasingly desirable—whether they've just met them or have been married to them for thirty years. So, if it's date night or the lights are low and the bed beckons, communication is a potent erotic overture to sex.

## WHAT IF I CAN'T LISTEN ANYMORE?

If you're stressed, distracted, have an appointment, or are tired, you can't just cut your lover off; as we've just cautioned, she'll get upset and bad things will happen. Instead, assure her that you're interested in what she is saying, make a time to continue the conversation later and be the one to bring it up. This lets her know you care and her concerns will be addressed.

Having to defer the conversation can still be a sore point for females, but women, be reasonable. Just because something's emotional, important to you, or a problem you feel you need to solve right now, doesn't mean it's a good time for your partner to hear you. This is particularly true of trying to process at night when he's dead tired and needs to go to sleep.

---

***CAUTION*** » *DO NOT TRY TO FORCE A MAN TO COMMUNICATE WHEN HE CAN'T. ALL YOU WILL ACCOMPLISH IS MUTUAL ALIENATION AND UPSET.*

---

Remember, ladies, stress blocks oxytocin. So if it's emotional connection you're after, pressuring him is counter-productive. Talking about it at a better time will always get better results.

# WHY DOES SHE ALWAY TALK TO HER GIRLFRIENDS WHEN SHE HAS A PROBLEM?

Who better to talk to? Girlfriends, can process anything, anytime, anywhere—exhausted or not. In addition, they respond differently to stress than guys do. While males are geared for "fight or flight"—repel the attacker or get the hell out, females automatically "tend and befriend" when they are in danger. The fair sex also gets the same "fight or flight" rush, but their oxytocin kicks in, overrides it and drives them to get seek help for their mutual survival.

Women can ask anyone they're close to, or even a stranger, to aid them if they're in a jam (which explains their irritating habit of asking for directions.) But there's a special bond between girlfriends and this bond creates a bulwark against physical and emotional stress.

---

*NOTE» OXYTOCIN IS A STRESS REDUCER: THE HIGHER IT GOES THE LOWER THE BLOOD PRESSURE.*

---

As the ladies share their triumphs, failures and struggles, their OT levels rise, making them feel calmer, more connected, and stronger. Supported by their allies, they can and will fight the good fight together.

---

*CAUTION» BE NICE TO YOUR LOVER'S GIRLFRIENDS. THE NEXT SOURCE OF STRESS THEY TALK ABOUT MAY BE YOU.*

---

## *TENDER HEARTS*

Girlfriends are especially good at helping each other because their OT makes them naturally empathetic, enabling them not only to hear what's being said, but also to feel it. This ability to walk in each other heels gives them a profound level of mutual understanding—one that you can't compete with.

Women respect and rely on their innate ability to recognize and feel what others feel. Their vital stream of emotional data informs their personal and social viewpoints, decisions and actions. On the other hand, men's T impacts the way they reason and show up in the world. If you recall from *Testosterone: The Big T,* the higher the T levels in the womb, the lower the empathy. Plus the OT blocking action of T reduces a guy's ability to experience mutual feeling. These divergent capacities can result in that enforcer vs. empath clash we spoke about.

*To him: she's too sensitive, overly emotional and a pushover.*

*To her: he's cold, unfeeling and punishing.*

Your baby's ability to relate puts her in tune with the entire spectrum of emotions, highs and lows and everything in between. Because she can feel people's pain, she is prone to be sympathetic and help them. If she acts cruelly, she can often feel what the recipient felt. The same is true if she's kind, which is a much nicer sensation.

You might not be programmed to be as emotionally responsive. Men often expect people to "man up", do what they have to do, be rewarded when they do and face the consequences when they don't.

Many of our female clients assume that their men should be as empathetic as they are, which leads them to conclude that their mates are insensitive and don't hear them. Meanwhile the guys get discouraged because they're doing their best. Really.

---

*CAUTION» LADIES, DON'T EXPECT YOUR PARTNER TO FEEL WHAT YOU'RE FEELING. HE PROBABLY CAN'T.*

---

Women, it's important to recognize how men are built and that it's not a defect if they're more into thought than emotion, and more into solving problems than hearing about them; they can still care about you, have helpful insights and offer constructive advice.

That being said, the male version of misguided expectations is for women to be more "rational" (read less emotional), which pisses their mates off because they don't see anything wrong with their logic.

Either of you deciding your partner is an idiot isn't just futile, it's also a lie. You might not necessarily have the same take on a situation, but that's life in the Big Relationship City. What matters is that you respect each other, agree to disagree when you're at odds and move on.

When it comes to the kids, it's common to hear the "too hard vs. too soft", "discipline vs. understanding" argument. You can't win this dispute, because both approaches are valuable when they're used appropriately. Once mom and dad accept it's not an either/or situation, they can make policies and coordinate their actions and the whole family benefits.

## MAKE LOVE, NOT WAR

**Have you heard about the oxytocin bomb?**
**You drop it on an area of violent conflict. Men throw down their guns and hug one another. Then they apologize, say it was their fault and clean up the mess.**

Oxytocin is the anti-aggression, anti-competition, anti-dominance and anti-hierarchy hormone. Partnership is the much-preferred system for someone who is focused on bonding, empathy and communication. Your "tending and befriending" mate enjoys getting input from many sources and collaborating when she's solving problems. As mentioned, she can compete for status in a rigid linear system and win, but she usually doesn't like it or get a chance to use her special community-oriented skills.

---

*CAUTION» IF YOU TRY TO BE THE COMMANDING OFFICER IN YOUR LOVE LIFE, PREPARE FOR HEAVY RESISTANCE.*

---

OT is democratic—one for all and all for one. T is hierarchal, king on top. A man could attempt to take charge because of his inbuilt awareness of a pecking order. Consciously or unconsciously he might be competing with or dominating his lover in order to be the Alpha and have to power to say "yes" or "no". He might also resent and resist her input because he misidentifies her intentions as an attempt to outrank him.

Historically, the tendency for men to dominate them has not escaped women's notice. However, your modern female does not have the legal and social constraints of the past and won't accept it. Healthy, happy relationships follow the wingman/wingwoman model: whoever has the skill, interest or experience in a given area takes the lead. And away they fly, watching each other's back, hitting their targets, bonded and loving. A round of oxytocin for all!

# THE TESTOSTERONE VS. OXYTOCIN COMPARISON CHART

| TESTOSTERONE | OXYTOCIN |
|---|---|
| **IN SEX** ||
| Drive for sex | Drive for connection and love |
| Wants more sex | Wants more connection and love |
| Makes less sensitive to the senses | Makes more sensitive to the senses |
| Doesn't need foreplay | Need for foreplay |
|  | Creates trust |
|  | Surges in orgasm |
|  | Causes contractions that enable a man to ejaculate |
| Blocks oxytocin after orgasm | Estrogen boosts oxytocin after orgasm |
| Drive for casual sex with many partners | Drive to bond and for relationship |
| **COMPETITION** ||
| Competitive drive to win | Drive for bonding and relationship |
| Testosterone is higher if males win, lower if they lose | Testosterone is not affected in females if they win or lose |
| **DOMINANCE** ||
| Drive to dominate and win | Drive for empathy, bonding and cooperation |

| TESTOSTERONE | OXYTOCIN |
|---|---|
| Drive to be the Alpha male | Community-oriented |
| Drive to get and keep high social status | |
| Hierarchal | |
| **AGGRESSION** | |
| The higher the testosterone, the more aggression | The higher the oxytocin, the less aggression |
| **SPEECH** | |
| Less verbal | More verbal |
| No dopamine (pleasure hormone) rush from talking | Gets a dopamine (pleasure hormone) rush from talking |
| Action-oriented | Communication-oriented |
| **RESPONSE TO STRESS** | |
| Fight or flight | Tend and befriend |
| **INDEPENDENCE** | |
| Drive for personal, independent action | Interdependent— drive for bonding, relationship, intimacy |
| Drive for space | Drive for togetherness |
| Focus on mission | Focus on relationship |

## THE OXYTOCIN QUIZ

**Rate your answers on the following scale:**

Almost Never = 1
Rarely = 2
Sometimes = 3
Often = 4
Almost Always =5

1. After orgasm, I like to lie there and cuddle with my sweetheart. _____

2. I am very sensitive and responsive to touch, sight, sound, taste and odors. _____

3. I have a strong drive for intimacy and bonding. _____

4. Relationships are a top priority and a measure of my success in life. _____

5. I'm partial to "togetherness" and want to spend a lot of time with my partner. _____

6. I am very empathetic and caring. _____

7. I love giving and helping others. _____

8. I get a lot of pleasure from conversation. _____

9. Talking calms me down and relieves my stress. _____

10. I prefer cooperation to competition. _____

**TOTAL _____**

**If you scored:**

- 40-50, you are very influenced by oxytocin.
- 10-20, you are minimally influenced by oxytocin.
- 21-39, you are in the middle range.

# ALL WEATHER OPERATIONS

**❚❚***When you think of all weather operations, you have to consider more than what the weather is in the atmosphere, i.e., is it rainy, snowy, cloudy or clear? You also have to take into consideration what the overall climate is. If you are in a desert area you have to be concerned about blowing sand. If you are in an arctic area, you have to consider the effect of the cold temperatures on the plane and the crew. If you are in a tropical area, how will the heat and the moisture affect things? If you are near salt water you have to take measures to prevent corrosion. In a fighter squadron, you may be deployed from one climate to another so you have to be prepared for whatever you encounter.***❚❚*

As men and women go from youthful bodies to aging bodies, we find ourselves confronting our own personal climate change. The same can be said for a young woman who goes from being fertile/lusty to being pregnant/nauseated, gives birth and then might experience postpartum depression. During each of these phases, the amount and balance of our testosterone, estrogen, progesterone, and oxytocin go up or down. Strange, new weather patterns become the norm.

Females are nothing if not complex. Their brains and bodies are intricately designed to procreate and their variable monthly weather is just the beginning. Huge hormonal changes in pregnancy and after delivery, unpredictably fluctuating hormones in perimenopause, and the hormonal dive in menopause create new and sometimes daunting challenges for your partner and for you.

Likewise, the slow, steady decrease in testosterone begins to hit males in their 40's. As your T goes down, your estrogen, progesterone and oxytocin gradually rise and you are in a new world—one you may have problems coping with. Now it might be your mate's turn to grapple with heavy clouds and unfamiliar headwinds.

If you or your woman is smack in the middle of one of these conditions, it's an obvious priority to learn about it. But do you really need to get briefed on future weather? Or a front that's passed?

Absolutely!

Knowing the forecast is always smart and debriefing brings clarity. Both create the understanding that will deepen your intimacy and strengthen your love, sex and relationship.

As pointed out in the Introduction, knowing what men and women go through boosts your relationship "IQ" and empowers you to deal more effectively with all the important people in your personal and work life.

So get ready. All Weather Operations, starting with pregnancy, are up ahead.

# CHAPTER FOUR

*From the first moment a woman learns that she's pregnant, she becomes a mother.*

## *PREGNANCY, POSTPARTUM AND MOTHERHOOD*

A pregnant woman goes through dramatic changes hormonally, physically, emotionally and spiritually, as she prepares for the miracle of your baby's birth. Her experience couldn't be more concrete: she feels the fetus growing, moving and kicking inside her.

It's different for men. The reality of a new life and becoming a father often doesn't become tangible until the baby is born. Sometimes it takes months to connect with the infant and feel like a dad. This disparity in experiences and points of view can be challenging to your relationship. So here are some basics to help you through those demanding times during pregnancy and after your baby is born.

## MOM SUPER-HORMONES

As your mate's attachment to her baby-to-be grows, she and her body develop new priorities. Now estrogen and progesterone become super-maternal as their main jobs become fostering and protecting the fetus. Both hormones, which are primarily produced by her placenta during gestation, soar as her pregnancy progresses. By the time your bundle of joy is born, your woman's *estriol* (the weakest form of estrogen and the main one associated with pregnancy) skyrockets up to a 1000 times higher than her normal amount. Progesterone levels rise to 300 times higher and oxytocin, the promoter of motherly bonding and love and the source of her contractions, shoots up 300 times at birth. Can you imagine what would happen if your testosterone rose 300 times or more? We're talking major weather fronts.

## THE THREE SEASONS

Pregnancy is divided into three trimesters: each is associated with the predictable development of the fetus and with the physical and emotional state your partner will be in.

---

**NOTE**» *NOW IS THE TIME TO GET A DOCTOR YOU COMPLETELY TRUST.*

---

## THE FIRST TRIMESTER: THE FIRST 12 WEEKS

You've just learned "we're pregnant." Atmospheric conditions are variable. For many couples, having children is a dream-come-true. If your lover/you are thrilled to have your baby, expect glorious sunshine. If she/you are surprised and uncertain, expect foggy and cloudy. If she/you are worried about your finances, your relationship, or your jobs, it could be wet, chilly and a chance of rain. So how much you want your baby and how you both react to her pregnancy will predict some of what the next nine months hold in store. But even the most delighted couple may find the emotional and physical weather trying.

---

*CAUTION» ALL STRESS CAN BE ALIENATING AND PREGNANCY CAN BE TRYING FOR BOTH MOM AND DAD. GOOD, CLEAR COMMUNICATION IS IMPERATIVE TO DRAW YOU CLOSER.*

---

We're putting this caution way up front in the chapter because if you can't talk about what's going on, problems will fester. We see it all the time. Couples come to counseling in crisis mode after years of not communicating. It's not uncommon for some of their issues to have begun in pregnancy or after birth. That's why we urge you not to wait. Each of you needs to take responsibility for expressing and listening to any worries, upsets, problems and needs—even if they seem petty, selfish, and unreasonable or make you feel vulnerable. It's only going to get harder with kids in your life, so this is a relationship muscle you need to develop ASAP. If you hit a wall, go to couple's counseling before it becomes a thousand feet high.

Keeping this in mind, here is our briefing on what conditions you might run into.

## WEATHER ADVISORY

**Q: Ever since my wife has been pregnant, she hasn't been able to go to bed at night without onion rings. Is this a normal craving?**

**A: It depends on what she's doing with them.**

Weird food cravings and aversions are two of the milder, more entertaining symptoms of pregnancy that show up in the first trimester. About 70% of women experience the less amusing nausea of "morning sickness," which actually occurs any time day or night. This can lead to throwing up, which is no fun at all. Why is this happening to your mate?

Her rapidly rising estrogen and progesterone are major players. Ditto for making her dizzy. Estrogen is solely responsible in these early months, however, for her newly swollen, tender breasts.

"I'm exhausted" will probably be a recurring refrain. Fondly nicknamed "Mother Nature's Prozac for Girls," progesterone sedates a woman in the third week of her period, making her feel tired, sleepy and fuzzy-brained. The huge amounts of progesterone during pregnancy, in addition to energy sapping low blood sugar, low blood pressure and higher production of blood, commonly lead to this first three months of fatigue. Progesterone's relaxant trait also slows down and messes with your mate's digestion and elimination, which can cause indigestion, heartburn and constipation.

On a positive note, most nausea, fatigue and dizziness usually subside, by the 12th week. The bad news is that the indigestion, heartburn and constipation can continue.

## VOLATILE WEATHER

**Q: My wife is three months pregnant and is so moody that she's sometimes borderline neurotic.**

**A: And your question is?**

A lot of women have mood swings in the first 12 weeks. They can be excited one day, weepy the next, have a deep sense of well-being, or be plagued by anxiety.

---

**NOTE**» *ESTROGEN MAGNIFIES THE EFFECTS OF CORTISOL, THE STRESS HORMONE.*

---

Now that your woman has a lot more estrogen, she can feel a lot more stressed. Aside from the physical problems, she has a whole bunch of new worries, a primary one being the baby's health. First time moms can be particularly anxious about doing everything right and knowing how to adjust to motherhood. Even veteran moms might worry about finances

133

and balancing the needs of her family and her career—concerns which might resonate with your own.

Another source of upset can be the fathers-to-be. Men don't necessarily become thoughtful the moment they find out their wives are pregnant. We've seen guys go absent or get irritated and impatient with their mates' needs. Some carry on as if nothing's changed; they continue aggravating, dangerous behavior like drinking, doing drugs, texting while driving, or being passive aggressive or uncontrollably angry. Others pick this time to have an affair. Afraid of their new responsibility, first time dads might hang out and drink more with their friends.

---

*WARNING» WOMEN DON'T FORGIVE AND FORGET BAD BEHAVIOR DURING THEIR PREGNANCY. WHAT YOU DO OR DON'T DO NOW WILL HAVE A LASTING IMPACT ON YOUR LOVE, SEX, AND RELATIONSHIP.*

---

❚❚ *When I was young, just graduated from college, I got my commission in the Air force and got married. I knew nothing about sex or relationships. When my wife got pregnant with our first child it was great and we were excited. When the second came along there wasn't as much enthusiasm, and by the time the third one came things were definitely different. I was not the cooperative component that my wife needed to support her in her pregnancy. She was feeling bad and withdrawing from me, which in turn drove me further away from her. All I was interested in was flying airplanes, racing cars and drinking in between.*

*❚❚In retrospect, I feel that my attitude during that period affected not only how my wife felt about me as our marriage deteriorated over the ensuing years but also affected the emotional nature of the child. If I had known more about what was happening to her as a result of the huge hormonal fluctuations she was experiencing, I could have been a better team player and things might have turned out differently. ❚❚*

There are also plenty of great, stand-up men who go through the pregnancy at their partner's side and do whatever they can to support their physical and emotional well-being. It's a no-brainer that their relationships are happier and healthier. Some can get so involved in sharing that they experience...

## WEIRD WEATHER

If you're among the lucky 25% of dads-to-be, you might take togetherness to the next level and start having some of the same symptoms as your mate—nausea, fatigue, and moodiness for starters. Going all the way, you can even develop your own belly and have labor pains. This high level of empathy is called the *Couvade syndrome* (from the French verb "to hatch"). Fascinatingly, men who suffer from it have lower levels of testosterone and higher levels of *prolactin*, the hormone that initiates the formation and secretion of mother's milk. On the plus side, studies suggest that men who feel this intensity of connection with their pregnant partner also connect deeply with their child.

Even if you're not one of these expectant fathers, Nature still built you to be involved physically—albeit to a much less degree. Your *prolactin* peaks in the weeks before birth, your testosterone goes down to its lowest point in the first days after it, and, understandably, your cortisol (the stress hormone) tops out during labor and delivery.

## SECOND TRIMESTER: WEEKS 13 TO 28 – SUNNY DAYS, CLEAR SKIES

This is usually the best part of a woman's pregnancy, so enjoy it while you can. For most moms, the progesterone driven nausea and exhaustion abate, so now they can eat and are energized, positive, and active and have a sense of well-being. This is also the time where you begin to see their pregnancy showing.

## PHYSICAL CHANGES

**Q: What is the grasp reflex?**

**A: The reaction of new fathers when they see a new mother's breasts.**

Those touchable breasts are the result of estrogen and progesterone stimulating the milk producing glands inside her breasts.

---

**NOTE**» *HER NIPPLES COULD GET TENDER FROM THIS POINT ON, SO EASY DOES IT.*

---

The huge increase of her hormones also cause the skin around her nipples, the line that runs down from her navel to her pubic bone, her labia, and parts of her face to get darker. Don't worry, this will fade after delivery.

As we noted earlier, estrogen increases blood circulation. When it goes to her skin, it makes her face glow—and her palms itch. It also causes red rashes and blotches. When it goes to her nose, it makes her mucous membranes swell, which in turn might mean everything from a stuffy or running nose to sinus congestion and headaches.

Besides the symptoms in her first trimester, her amped-up progesterone can now cause:

- Kidney and bladder infection, which is dangerous to the fetus

- Head aches

- Blurry vision

This is also the time when your mate begins to get a belly as her uterus expands to make room for the baby. She'll be gaining about three to four pounds a month from now on.

## CAN WE HAVE SEX DURING PREGNANCY?

The short answer is an enthusiastic "yes!" The longer answer has a lot of "depends" in it. Although most women like sex during pregnancy, the research generally finds that both how much and how often they want it decreases from their norm. The nausea and fatigue of the first trimester aren't exactly conducive to erotic thoughts. Neither are the bulk, backaches, breathing problems and crankiness of the third. So the mild, sunny days of the second trimester are usually your best bet.

---

*NOTE» A CONSIDERABLE NUMBER OF WOMEN ACTUALLY ENJOY MORE SATISFACTION DURING THEIR PREGNANCIES.*

---

Feeling fat and unattractive are not helpful to the desire to couple, and some women struggle with their body image as their bellies expand.

---

*NOTE» ENCOURAGE HER SELF–ESTEEM. REMIND HER HOW PRETTY SHE IS AND HOW MUCH YOU LOVE HER.*

---

Obviously don't try to be sexual if she's feeling crappy. Even if she's doing fine, you need to ask her how she'd like you to express your love and affection. There might be times that snuggling and hugging and nothing more might connect you. Needless to say, if you get frustrated, pleasure yourself.

## THE THIRD TRIMESTER: WEEKS 29 TO 40

Your mate's breasts are about two pounds heavier and there's 25-35 pounds more of her to love by the time she delivers. Thus, sex can get tricky; the impact of backaches, swelling in her arms, feet and legs, shortness of breath, heartburn, hemorrhoids and other discomforts are definitely anti-aphrodisiac.

---

*NOTE» SOME WOMEN HOWEVER, MAY REALLY WANT TO MAKE LOVE, SO ASK.*

---

This is the trimester when the baby is moving a lot and can hear sounds, and mom and dad may be talking to it. The reality of their fully formed kid in their lover's belly may make some men feel weird about having sex. Doctors, however, universally agree sex won't hurt the baby. And your mutual pleasure and intimacy will make you both feel closer and better.

---

*WARNING» JUST DON'T PUT PRESSURE ON HER UTERUS OR YOUR FULL WEIGHT ON HER BELLY DURING SEX.*

---

Remember oxytocin, the love and bonding hormone, is always on alert to help you create a connection with your woman. Talking, eye-gazing, and physical contact, like hugging, stroking and kissing release it into her bloodstream, lowering her blood pressure and creating a feeling of euphoria and a tender attachment to you. So will erotically simulating her nipples, if they're not too sensitive. Orgasm releases oxytocin big time for both of you. But even if neither of you want sex, you or your lover might still want affectionate contact. So you use your oxytocin love and bonding tool kit and connect.

---

*NOTE» RELEASING OXYTOCIN CHANGES THE ACTIVITY IN YOUR MATE'S UTERUS. STIMULATING HER BREAST OR CLITORIS LATE IN PREGNANCY CAN NATURALLY PROMOTE LABOR AND DELIVERY.*

---

Other couples may find intercourse awkward and not be able to find a position that works for both. Worry not. Since most women experience orgasm from clitoral stimulation, lots of foreplay, oral sex, fingers and vibrators can do the trick. And she can return the favor.

---

*NOTE» DUE TO THEIR HORMONAL CHANGES, WOMEN'S SECRETIONS MIGHT TASTE AND SMELL STRONGER, TURNING SOME MEN OFF.*

---

An infection or changes in bacteria could be the reason, so using probiotics, which support the growth of healthy bacteria and keep her vagina more acidic, might help. If the problem doesn't resolve, she needs to have her doctor do a culture to check what's going on.

## *THIRD TRIMESTER WEATHER REPORT*

Cranky and tired with a chance of anxiety and feeling overwhelmed. Don't get impatient if she starts worrying about the pain of childbirth, how long it will last and the health of the baby. It's natural. Also, you've probably both reached the point where you just want to get it over with and have the baby.

## FINAL TIPS

**Q: Is there any reason I have to be in the delivery room while my wife is in labor?**
**A: Not unless the word "alimony" means anything to you.**

Nowadays women expect their mates to be involved and share in the on-going experience of their pregnancy. Here are some ways to support your lover and witness a miracle in the making.

## DOCTOR VISITS

- Accompany your mate on some doctor's appointments to get a sense of what's going on. Ask the doctor questions, be informed, and if there's a problem, discover why your partner might be anxious. That way you can become a worrywart too.

- Share in the excitement and wonder. By week seven, your baby has begun to develop its eyes, ears, nose, heart and other organs. By week eight it starts moving and you can hear its heartbeat in an ultrasound. Listen together. Maybe this is your first indication that it's really alive.

- By week ten, you've a got tiny, completely developed baby. Go to the doctor in week 12 or 13 when it's big enough to see in a sonogram. That's when you can tell if it's a boy or girl.

- Take birthing classes with her, so you can help.

    Love and oxytocin all around.

## *SEND IN THE REINFORCEMENTS*

Your wife's delivery could be that rare occasion where you enthusiastically relinquish control and hire a *doula* (Gk. woman's servant) to be the in-charge labor coach. She's the non-medical part of your support team. While your doctor and nurse or midwife deliver the baby, she gives your partner constant, nurturing attention during labor by massaging her, using techniques to ease her pain that could include repositioning her body, breathing and visualization techniques, and helping her bathe or shower (water is the "doula's epidural"). She also joins you in cheering her on and giving her that all-important, stress-reducing emotional comfort.

So if you want to help, but don't think you're up to doing the job by yourself, don't worry. The doula is an encouraging guide who shows you what you can do to be useful. She also provides the space for you to simply be at your mate's side, showering her with love and sharing the wonder of your baby's birth—which are your most important jobs.

## MISSION ACCOMPLISHED: BIRTH – WEEKS 37 TO 42

Whether you decide to use a doula or not, you are now at zero hour.

**Q: Our childbirth instructor says it's not pain my mate will feel during labor, but pressure. Is she right?**

**A: Yes, in the same way that a tornado might be called an air current.**

So here you are, holding your lover's hand, counting and coaching her through the delivery. She's screaming in pain and laboring to push your kid out. You're trying to keep your cool and support her. Knowing what's going on helps.

## STANDARD OPERATING PROCEDURES: THE WAY NATURE PLANNED IT

Mother Nature, the Big Mama to all of us, ensures the baby's birth and the new mother's bond to it by a brilliant, efficient use of her "maternal hormone." Doing double duty, oxytocin causes the powerful contractions that push the baby out and the tremendous elation, love and connection to her infant after delivery. This is how it works:

- The oxytocin receptors in your mate's uterus gradually increase during her pregnancy, then soar during labor.

- Contraction-preventing progesterone dives.

- Oxytocin, which means "swift birth", takes the controls.

- Oxytocin triggers forceful contractions that help to thin and dilate her cervix (the bottom part of her uterus) and move your baby down the birth canal and out into your family.

- Baby does its part too. By pressing against the cervix and the tissues of the pelvic floor, it triggers the oxytocin and those powerful contractions that expel it and its placenta.

- Oxytocin also prevents bleeding at the placenta site.

## OXYTOCIN SUPERNOVA

A huge surge of oxytocin—300 times more than normal—inundates the mother's brain and body at birth and creates the legendary elation, profound love, and the deep, lasting tie with her newborn. This will affect everyone in your family till death do you part.

Even after birth, your woman's levels of natural oxytocin continue to be very high, making that love connection stronger.

Watching or participating in your baby's birth, holding it and looking into its eyes may also stimulate your oxytocin and make you fall in love.

## NON-STANDARD OPERATIONS

Your mate might not get to experience the classic vaginal birth due to threats to her or your baby's health.

Modern medicine has developed life-saving interventions to address these threats, but they can hurry Mother Nature along, or bypass her completely. In some cases, the powerful oxytocin engine is completely sidestepped. Changing a natural process has its own set of short or long-term risks and consequences. Of course you've got to do what you've got to do in an emergency, but there is growing concern about overdependence and overuse of these interventions. Therefore, choices need to be carefully weighed.

## INDUCING LABOR

*Inducing labor* means using any process to instigate labor before it spontaneously starts.

---

**NOTE**» *ONE IN FIVE BIRTHS IS INDUCED.*

---

Why is that? Sometimes Nature needs a helping hand because complications threaten the health of mom or baby. After 42 weeks, risks to mother and fetus increase greatly, so obstetricians often induce labor between the 41st and 42nd week. Other health risks, like the mom's high blood pressure, toxemia, gestational diabetes, bleeding or an infection in her uterus, the baby's abnormal development or heartbeat, or its being positioned sideways in the uterus also lead to speeding up the birth. The doctors normally use various mechanical techniques and/or *Pitocin*, a synthetic oxytocin, to do the job.

## IS PITOCIN THE SAME AS NATURAL OXYTOCIN?

No. Pitocin doesn't penetrate the brain and create the supernova oxytocin boost and intense bonding at birth. Delivered intravenously, what it does do is gradually stimulate your mate's contractions until they're strong and frequent enough for the baby to be delivered. It's used to start labor or strengthen it if it's slowed down or stalled.

---

**WARNING»** IT MUST BE USED IF LABOR HAS STALLED BECAUSE IF DELIVERY DOESN'T HAPPEN, THE MOTHER AND THE FETUS COULD BE IN DANGER.

---

## CLOUD SEEDING

Inducing labor is skyrocketing, but not only because of health risks. More and more women or their obstetricians opt to start labor earlier to fit their schedules or to make sure the mom-to-be will get to the hospital in time if she lives far away from it. As convenient as delivery appointments might be, there are side effects to consider—especially if Pitocin is used.

One problem is that Pitocin's contractions can be stronger and more frequent than those caused by your mate's own oxytocin. Although that doesn't bother some women, others find that their labor is harder, longer and more painful. The faster contractions can also decrease the oxygen your fetus gets and can cause it to become distressed and unable to cope with the demands of labor. That means it needs to be delivered by *Caesarean-section (C-section)*. More on C-Sections very shortly. And, complications from Pitocin require other interventions, all with their own set of risks. Very rarely, synthetic oxytocin can create problems that are potentially fatal to mother and child.

Until recently it was assumed Pitocin didn't affect baby after the blessed event. Not so, says Dr. Michael S. Tsimis and his team of researchers. They analyzed data from 3000 women whose full-term deliveries were induced or augmented by Pitocin and found:

---

*CAUTION» NEWBORNS WHOSE MOMS USED PITOCIN SPENT AT LEAST 24 HOURS IN THE NEONATAL INTENSIVE CARE UNIT AND HAD LOWER APGAR SCORES.*

---

Okay, time to add another word to your required baby vocabulary. *APGAR* measures Appearance (color), Pulse (heartbeat), Grimace (reflex), Activity (muscle tone), and Respiration (breathing). An infant whose score begins at eight, on a one to ten scale, is considered healthy.

---

*CAUTION» NEWBORNS WHOSE MOMS WERE ASSISTED BY PITOCIN SCORED SEVEN AND UNDER.*

---

Bottom line is, you and your mate need to assess the pros and cons of induction and of using Pitocin. But even if you nix both, you may find that a routine medical procedure, such as getting an epidural, triggers the need for them.

## EPIDURALS

**Q: When is the best time for a woman to get an epidural?**

**A: Right after she finds out she's pregnant.**

Jokes aside, most women prefer a totally natural birth, but the pain of labor can become so intense that they request this common and effective painkiller. A good thing, right? Yes and no. Potential side effects include:

- *A sudden drop of blood pressure*

- *A longer labor*

- *Difficulty pushing the baby out*

- *Fever*

If any of these situations occur, new procedures have to be used which can lead directly, or through a chain of interventions, to your doctor inducing labor or doing a C-section.

## C-SECTIONS

There's even a greater chance your mate will have a C-section than induced labor. How does it affect her? Since Pitocin can't cross the blood-brain barrier, she won't get the same euphoric oxytocin rush and resulting intense bonding. The surgical procedure of making incisions in the mother's abdomen and uterus and then removing the baby completely bypasses the natural process.

Although C-sections are relatively safe, surgery is surgery, so there's a greater risk of complications for mom and baby than there is for a vaginal birth. Your partner could have blood clots, wound infections, excessive bleeding, or damage to her bladder or uterus. If the incision leaves a weak spot in the wall of her uterus, she might not be able to have a vaginal birth later. It will also take her longer to recover than if she gave birth vaginally.

---

*CAUTION» C-SECTIONS TRIPLE THE RISK OF DEATH FOR MOTHERS AND ALMOST TRIPLES THE RATE OF FATALITIES IN NEWBORNS.*

---

However, like inducing labor, health risks can make it imperative.

---

*NOTE» ACCORDING TO THE WORLD HEALTH ORGANIZATION, BETWEEN 5%-15% OF C-SECTIONS ARE CRUCIAL; THERE ARE NO HEALTH BENEFITS AFTER THAT.*

---

Yet the C-section rate is 33% in the United States. So, what's up? Given the increased risks, why so many?

- There are health risks to the mother or fetus that are known beforehand or arise during delivery.

- Interventions beget interventions that lead to a C-section.

- Is your mate plump? About 73% of American women are overweight and 32% are obese. A heavier mom might need a C-section to protect her bigger baby from fracturing its collarbone or getting paralysis in its arm in the vaginal canal.

---

*CAUTION» A C-SECTION IS A MAJOR OPERATION FOR AN OBESE WOMAN AND CARRIES GREATER RISKS FOR HER AND BABY THAN FOR A SLIMMER WOMAN.*

---

- Is your woman over 35? If so, she's more at risk for complications, and therefore more at risk for getting a C-section. Nowadays more educated, career-oriented women are marrying and having kids later in life. In fact, moms over 35 are having more kids than teenagers, and the only age group whose birthrate rose in 2010 was women over 40.

---

*NOTE» ABOUT ONE IN SEVEN, OR 14% OF OUR NEW CITIZENS, ARE BORN TO OLDER MOMS.*

---

- Did your mate need fertility treatments to get pregnant? Did they result in twins? Triplets? MORE??? Multiple births increase the need to have a C-section.

- Some women and obstetricians elect to have "C-sections-On- Demand" for convenience, or other non-health related issues.

---

*NOTE» DEPENDING ON HER AGE AND THE CIRCUMSTANCES OF HER FIRST BIRTH, MOST DOCTORS WILL ALLOW A WOMAN TO HAVE A NATURAL BIRTH AFTER A C-SECTION.*

---

## IS "CONVENIENCE" A GOOD MOTIVE TO HAVE AN EARLY DELIVERY?

No. The American College of Obstetricians and Gynecologists defines full-term birth as 39-41 weeks and your baby needs every bit of it to develop properly.

---

*WARNING» EARLY-ELECTIVE DELIVERY CREATES THE RISK OF COMPLICATIONS, INCLUDING BREATHING AND FEEDING PROBLEMS, INFECTIONS, AND A 50% INCREASE IN INFANT MORTALITY.*

---

It also commonly leads to a C-section, which as you've just read and will read more about, is fraught with its own potential risks to both mother and fetus.

So why do it? Common sense dictates avoiding these dangers if you can. Factor in the approximately one billion dollars a year in added healthcare costs, and prohibiting early-elective delivery seems to be a no-brainer. That's why employers who pay for health insurance, patient-safety advocates and U.S government officials are pressuring doctors and hospitals to end the practice. And when reason doesn't prevail, money talks: a growing number of insurance companies and government health programs won't pay doctors or hospitals for it.

This anti-early elective coalition is working. Although there are still U.S. hospitals where 20%-30% of all births are "convenience" deliveries, there has been a sharp decline across the country.

---

**NOTE**» *EARLY-ELECTIVE DELIVERIES IN 1000 REPORTING HOSPITALS FELL FROM 17% IN 2010 TO 4.6% IN 2013.*

---

Well done, warriors!

Now, back to C-section issues.

## WEATHER ALERT

Another potential difficulty from C-sections could show up in mother-infant bonding. One study followed a dozen women for a month after birth, and did MRI brain scans to see if natural delivery vs. a C-section affected their responsiveness to their infants' cries. The six with vaginal births had more activity in the areas of the brain linked to emotions and parenting and were more responsive to their infant's cries than the six who had elective C-sections. Four months later, the MRIs showed the gap was still there, but was lessening. The researchers theorized that the oxytocin released in a natural delivery made the difference.

## WHAT CAN YOU DO?

Birth isn't what it used to be, so be prepared for a lot of different situations and choices—and for being by your mate's side, emotionally and physically through them.

One practical action you can take if she has induced labor or a C-section is to get her nursing right away in the recovery room.

---

*NOTE» BREASTFEEDING IS THE BIGGEST ONGOING STIMULATOR OF OXYTOCIN.*

---

As the baby sucks her mother's nipples, oxytocin is stimulated, making her milk flow and engendering more loving, nurturing and bonding feelings.

Even if your mate can't breastfeed right away, make sure she holds your baby ASAP. Touch stimulates oxytocin in mother and child. Research has found that how long mom and newborn are separated after birth, as well as suckling soon afterward, affects how much they will bond. Let your doctor know that you want to keep your baby in her hospital room.

---

*NOTE» WOMEN TAUGHT BY DOULAS HOW TO NURSE HAVE BETTER RATES OF BREASTFEEDING AFTER SIX WEEKS (51%) COMPARED TO THOSE WHO WEREN'T (29%).*

---

Studies and reviews also confirm some other remarkable benefits of having a doula as a member of the birth team, including:

- A 25% drop in the length of labor

- A 40% drop in Pitocin use

- A 60% drop in requests for epidurals

- A 30% drop in the use of pain relief medication

- A whopping 50% drop in C-sections

It just goes to show how powerful TLC and continuous support are for mom during labor and delivery. Depending on the weather after birth, you might want to use a doula to help with physical and emotional support at home.

## OVERCAST, WITH A HIGH CHANCE OF SHOWERS

Your partner's estrogen and *progesterone* nose-dive to the level they were before pregnancy within the first 24 hours after delivery. This emotional crash affects about 80% of mothers and is fondly referred to as "baby blues." *Postpartum*. From delivery to six weeks after birth can lead to:

- Sadness

- Tearfulness

- Anxiety

- Irritability

- Sleeplessness

- Restlessness

Fortunately this too shall probably pass within a couple of days to two to three weeks. Meanwhile, repeat after us: "Sleep, rest, sleep, rest". Given the fact your mate is often up nursing, you can support her by removing stress and letting her get what little sleep and rest she can.

## SEVERE STORMS

If your wife's blues linger more than a month or you find her to be horribly depressed for six months to a year after she gives birth, she belongs to the about 10%-25% of new mothers who experience *postpartum depression (PPD)*. She'll feel the predictable symptoms of depression such as:

- Anxiety

- Sadness

- Irritability

- A loss of energy

- A loss of pleasure in what she does

- Sleeping and eating problems

- A reduced sex drive

---

*CAUTION»* *ACCORDING TO THE NATIONAL INSTITUTES OF HEALTH, MOTHERS WHO DIDN'T BREASTFEED OR STOPPED AFTER A SHORT TIME HAD A HIGHER RISK OF PPD.*

---

We assume that mothers love their kids, but what distinguishes PPD from depression in general is how the woman's connection with her infant suffers. She is less nurturing, emotionally available, and consistent in taking care of her newborn and expresses more negativity toward it and the job of being a mother.

PPD is serious. Call in the troops to support her—friends, family, doctors, clergy, doulas and therapists. Since most women are naturally empathetic, a PPD support group could really help.

There are also medications, natural substances, vitamins and a nutritious diet that can assist her. And of course, don't create stress for her and let her rest and sleep, rest and sleep.

## DIRE BLIZZARD

You've probably seen news stories about mothers hearing voices that command them to kill their kids. Such postpartum psychosis develops in 1%-2% of postpartum mothers. It doesn't emerge until several weeks or months after the baby is born. These poor women lose their reason, and often have dark fantasies and hallucinations that focus on hurting themselves or their children. This is war. Run, do not walk, to get medical and psychiatric help.

---

***WARNING*** » *AT LEAST 50% OF WOMEN WHO HAD PPD WILL HAVE IT AGAIN WHEN THEY HAVE ANOTHER CHILD.*

---

Given this fact, you need to carefully weigh the pros and cons of having more kids. It may not be the greatest good for all concerned. If you do decide to go ahead, you need to have a plan in place for how you will take care of your mate, her medical needs, your children and yourself. It's a big responsibility.

## DOES INDUCING BIRTH OR HAVING A C-SECTION INCREASE THE RISK FOR POSTPARTUM DEPRESSION?

The answer is a definite "no, yes and maybe." Most research has not found a connection between the surging oxytocin of a natural vaginal birth, using synthetic oxytocin, or bypassing it altogether in a C-section. There are, however, other studies that do find a clear-cut connection, and others that think there could be one. This is a growing science, so stay tuned and decide what's true for you from your own experience.

## ARE THERE CLEAR-CUT CAUSES OF PPD?

Yes, and you don't need radar to detect them. Having an unwanted pregnancy, a traumatic birth, worries about money, her job or her relationship with you are all obvious to the naked eye. If you, family and friends don't give your woman adequate emotional or physical support, it's understandable that she might feel overwhelmed, despairing and hopeless.

---

**WARNING**» *GIVE HER THE SUPPORT AND BE PROACTIVE IN SOLVING THE PROBLEMS. YOUR LOVER'S HEALTH, YOUR MARRIAGE AND YOUR CHILD'S WELFARE ARE AT STAKE.*

---

## SEVERE WEATHER FOR DADS

Pride, excitement and joy! That's supposed to be the forecast for new dads. But, like getting a bird strike on takeoff, dads can be hit with a frightening condition instead that puts them, their relationships and their kids in danger: *Paternal Postpartum Depression (PPPD).* And it's more common than you might think.

---

**NOTE**» *14.1 % OF U.S. DADS SUFFER PRENATAL OR POSTPARTUM DEPRESSION COMPARED TO 8.2% WORLDWIDE.*

---

Since his mate is the one doing the heavy lifting and going through the huge hormonal changes, dad generally either doesn't recognize or feel entitled to being depressed. Yet PPPD can start as early as his mate's first trimester and last as long as a year after their child's birth. Months three to six postpartum are the most vulnerable ones; that's when about a quarter of PPPD fathers get the baby blues.

## IS THERE A HORMONAL COMPONENT?

Low T is linked to depression in men, and the sharply falling levels of testosterone after birth, plus a rise in estrogen levels, can trigger ongoing miserable feelings. Good news: T levels rise gradually to their former levels in about a year.

## ARE THERE CLEAR CUT REASONS?

Just like mom, sleep deprivation, economic stress, relationship problems, lack of support, and feeling trapped or overwhelmed can cause debilitating unhappiness. If his mate is suffering from postpartum depression, guess what? He's 50% more likely to as well. Then there's the jealousy factor. A guy can resent mom's focused attention on her newborn and for not having the time or strength to take care of both the baby and him. Their sex life can nose dive because she doesn't feel like having sex, but he needs it as much as ever.

## TURBULENT HOUSEHOLDS

It's rough weather when either mate is depressed and worse if they both are. What also makes things hard is when men, who don't usually rank high in emotional self-awareness, and women, who usually do, misidentify it. That happens because males and females have different symptoms: women are predisposed by their estrogen to get sad, hopeless, tearful and withdrawn; men's blues are more in line with their testosterone. Signs that he's clinically depressed are:

- Anger

- Irritability

- Not showing up as a mate or dad

- Constantly working

- Drinking or doing drugs

- Having an affair

While women's misery is passive and doesn't seem like a willful attack, men's aggressive behavior does.

---

**WARNING**» *LADIES, AS SELFISH OR CRUEL AS HIS ACTIONS SEEM, AS PAINFUL AND BRUISING AS THEY ARE, IT'S VITAL TO UNDERSTAND THAT HE'S HAVING A MENTAL HEALTH CRISIS, IS OUT OF CONTROL AND NEEDS HELP.*

---

If a deeply unhappy father doesn't get help, the emergency can escalate into physical abuse of you or your child.

---

**WARNING**» *ONE STUDY FOUND THAT DEPRESSED FATHERS SPANKED THEIR ONE-YEAR OLDS 4 TIMES MORE THAN NON-DEPRESSED DADS.*

---

The long-term forecast for the kids of depressed dads is dire: when they're three years old, they have more emotional and behavioral problems, and when they're seven, they have more psychiatric illnesses than other children.

## DEF CON 2

Guys, you need to immediately initiate Defense Condition 2 (all crews mobilized and ready to launch) as soon as you see Paternal Postpartum symptoms. The longer it lasts, the more dangerous it becomes, so it's imperative to bypass your T-driven "I'll handle it myself," way of thinking. It's going to take a dedicated team as well as a warrior's determination to overcome your depression.

Therefore, you need to employ the same support systems that mothers with Postpartum Depression use: friends, family, doctors, clergy, support groups and therapists. It's crucial that you talk about what's going on to get insight and effective strategies, as well as the backup to put them into action. There are also medications, natural substances, vitamins and a nutritious diet that can assist you.

And let's not forget sleep, the lack of which is a major source of PPPD. Cutting down on caffeine and occasionally taking a sleeping pill is something you can do yourself. However hard it may be, you and your mate have to figure out solutions that allow the rest that's required to keep you both sane.

## SUNNY AND WARM

**Q: Our baby was born last week. When will my wife begin to feel and act normal again?**

**A: When the kids are in college.**

Okay, here's the classic mom—loving, protective, and putting her kid's welfare before her own. Mother Nature ensures enduring interest and commitment through her Queen of Hearts, oxytocin; it's all about love and bonding.

Often dubbed "the maternal hormone," oxytocin promotes focus, attentiveness, caring, love and connection with the baby. Nature keeps it pumping through all the normal nurturing activities. Breast feeding is a huge source of oxytocin and eye gazing, hugging, cuddling, and touching all activate it and make mom fall in love. In fact, despite the lack of sleep an infant demands, women can feel incredible bliss.

## WHAT ABOUT BABY?

Your infant's oxytocin peaks at birth and is high for at least four days after it. Mother Nature is nothing if not efficient, so the same actions that stimulate mom's oxytocin, stimulates baby's suckling, touching, eye contact and cuddling. Plus, the love hormone is present in breast milk.

## WHAT ABOUT DAD?

As you may have observed, dads can fall in love with baby too, thanks in part to more availability of the bonding hormone. Although testosterone blocks oxytocin, T goes down when men are in a committed relationship and goes down even further when they have kids. So, with baby on the scene, guys are more open to oxytocin's effects—especially if they look into its eyes, cuddle, kiss it, etc. Women, encourage the connection.

Some moms appropriate the baby as only "theirs," and forbid the father to care for it or make decisions about its welfare.

---

**WARNING**» MARGINALIZING DAD DESTROYS THE FAMILY DYNAMIC AND CAN LEAD TO ALIENATION AND DIVORCE.

---

## ARE SOME WOMEN MORE NATURALLY MATERNAL?

Just as there are high-T men and high-E women, there may be high oxytocin women who are more hormonally geared toward motherhood. A recent study revealed that women with higher oxytocin levels in their first trimester were more attentive, positive, affectionate and attached to their babies than those with less.

The same was true of moms with higher oxytocin levels throughout gestation and for a month after birth. Men, take note: aside from the joyful connections listed above, the higher oxytocin moms were constantly on alert about their baby's safety when they weren't with it and looked in on it more than the moms with less oxytocin. Sound familiar? It could be the start of the famous "you're overprotective", vs." you're reckless", mom/dad conflict.

## WILL SHE WANT SEX AFTER THE BABY IS BORN?

Although some women have normal or stronger libidos after childbirth, most lose interest in sex for a while. The question is "how long is a while"? Doctors generally agree that it's okay to have intercourse six weeks after childbirth but if you're eagerly counting down to "I-Day," you could be disappointed; some women heal faster than others and your mate might need more time. Three months is the next target date because her hormones should be back to normal and she ought to be getting her period by then—unless she's breastfeeding. With her estrogen and testosterone rising at ovulation, she's supposed to be turned on, right? Not necessarily.

---

**NOTE**» *ONE STUDY FOUND THAT AT THE THREE-MONTH POINT, 20% OF POSTPARTUM WOMEN HAD LITTLE OR NO DESIRE FOR SEX AND 21% HAD COMPLETELY LOST THEIR LIBIDO OR WERE REPELLED BY SEX.*

---

Some physicians report it can take many more months, even a year before most moms want sex again. If you take a look at online forums, you'll see post after post of worried women who have lost interest for one to four or more years. So yes, this can be a problem for some couples. We'll tell you what you can do about it shortly.

## THE DAMAGE

We see the repercussions in alienated couples. Some are new parents, but most wait years to get help; they trace the start of their dismal sex life to the postpartum period. Sometimes they did fine with the first baby, but began having trouble after a subsequent birth.

Usually, the men's complaints are remarkably identical. Ditto for the women's. The dads are angry, resentful or hopeless about not having sex. They accuse their mates of consciously preventing sex, marginalizing them and dismissing their needs. Hormones aside, the mothers blame their partners for turning them off in postpartum by insisting on sex that hurts, ignoring their exhaustion, not sufficiently helping them with their workload, refusing to be romantic and continuing to act out some of the same bad behavior. While it is true that the women need to recognize their own failings, they do have a point: their mates don't see a cause and effect connection between what they're doing and what they're not getting. We do, so we're going to spell it out. If you want good sex, pay attention.

## PHYSICAL

When a woman says she's in pain, believe her. She's not making it up; it's not in her head. It doesn't mean it's a little pain, or she'll get over it if you continue. It means stop what you're doing and don't keep pushing her to have inter-course. Why would she be in pain? Here are a few reasons:

- Giving birth is physically arduous and traumatic. Her vagina is tender and sore.

- Estrogen levels go down after birth, resulting in vaginal dryness. If the mom is nursing, they go down even further. A dry vagina is not a happy one and will hurt if you stick anything into it, so you need to use lots of lube. If her vagina is still dry, your mate needs to get a low-dose prescription estrogen cream to aid the lubrication and elasticity of her vaginal tissue.

---

***NOTE***» *NEITHER OF THESE SOLUTIONS MEANS YOU SKIP FOREPLAY. YOU STILL NEED TO TURN HER ON.*

---

Remember that most women climax from clitoral simulation, not intercourse, so you can pleasure her orally or with your fingers. And be open to having her give you oral sex or masturbating you until she's ready for intercourse.

- She might have stitches from a C-section that need to heal.

- She might have jagged tears from pushing the baby out and they might form scar tissue.

- She had an episiotomy (a cut vagina so the baby's head can come out). That area can be sore or swollen or the cut might have formed keloid scars, which can be excruciatingly painful during intercourse.

- The muscles in her lower belly that are supposed to hold her pelvic organs have become weak or are stretched from giving birth. The result is that her uterus or bladder slips out of place (prolapsed) and presses against the walls of her vagina. Pressure on her belly can make it worse and intercourse can cause pain.

---

**WARNING**» *LADIES, YOU MUST SEE A DOCTOR IF INTERCOURSE IS PAINFUL. FIND OUT WHAT'S GOING ON AND FIX IT.*

---

## EXTREME EXHAUSTION

Taking care of an infant is exhausting for all concerned, but especially mom because she's depleted from the birth and usually has the majority of responsibility for the baby. Sleep deprivation from waking up every few hours to feed it can turn her into a sleepwalker during the day. A lot of dads are great about taking turns and doing chores to help out, but some men limit their assistance or refuse to pitch in. Why? Because they think:

- She's the mom; it's her job
- If she isn't employed, she gets plenty of time to rest
- I'm working harder
- I've worked all day and I just want to rest when I come home
- I help her enough

So THAT'S Why They Do That

Do any of these beliefs sound chauvinistic or like they're devaluing the effort it takes to be a mother and take care of a family? We can safely say they do to women. Guys frequently complain that women aren't direct, so they don't know what they want. In this case, it's very clear. If your mate asks for your help, she needs your help. If you want to make her happy and have her willing to make you happy, give it to her.

---

**WARNING»** *DO NOT, AS SOME OF OUR CLIENTS DO, INSULT HER BY PUTTING HER DOWN, OR INFERRING SHE'S LAZY OR INCOMPETENT FOR NOT BEING ABLE TO DO MORE BY HERSELF.*

---

If you do, you will have a partner who is angry and resentful as well as too worn out to make love. She will not want to talk to you, much less have sex with you. On the other hand, if you roll up your sleeves, give her time to rest, sleep and have a moment for herself, you'll create the conditions for a loving relationship and a healthy sex life. You'll also make it easier for her to feel good about herself, which is good for her libido.

## BODY IMAGE

Mom is tired, feels bloated, has gained weight, and doesn't have much or any time to groom herself. She looks fatigued, isn't wearing makeup, needs to wash her hair and

168

her blouse is drool-stained. Does this make her feel sexy? Probably not.

A woman gets demoralized when she feels unattractive and that can affect her libido. Case in point: Has your lover ever asked you if she looks fat? Or old? Or any other question about her appearance? Warning sirens go off in your head. Instantly, you reply "No"! Answering "yes" would mean shooting a bullet in the heart of romance and no sex that night. Using that same wisdom and those survival skills, you need to reassure your postpartum partner how much you love her and how desirable she is to you. And not just before you want to make love—you want her to know on a daily basis.

Moms can also worry that not looking good will turn their partners off—despite evidence that dads are desperate to make love with them.

---

*WARNING*» *LADIES, YOU'VE GOT TO HEAR WHAT YOUR MEN ARE SAYING. YOUR BODY DOES NOT TURN THEM OFF; THEY GET TURNED OFF BY YOUR NOT TOUCHING, CONNECTING AND HAVING SEX WITH THEM.*

---

Another strategy to boost your mate's morale is to give her "me-time". Encourage her to take a scented bath, get a pedicure, go to yoga, or whatever makes her feel more feminine.

---

*NOTE» LADIES, AS HARD AS IT MAY SEEM,*
*YOU NEED TO MAKE TAKING CARE OF*
*YOURSELF A PRIORITY, FOR YOU, YOUR MATE*
*AND FOR YOUR RELATIONSHIP.*

---

## BABY FIRST

One reason some moms might not take time for themselves is that they believe it's their duty to put their children first, before anyone and everything else. If you are one of these mothers, you need to hear this:

---

*WARNING» YOUR THINKING IS FLAWED*
*AND WILL WIND UP GETTING YOU THE*
*SAME RESULTS THAT MEN GET WHEN*
*THEY PUT THEIR CAREERS FIRST—*
*DISSATISFIED, UNHAPPY MATES AND BROKEN*
*RELATIONSHIPS.*

---

Men, understandably, resent being demoted to second place and having their needs, such as sex, ignored or trivialized.

Yes, the baby does need most of your attention for a while but remember that it is coming into your life to be part of the family, not to replace its father in importance. We like using the analogy of mom and dad being co-pilots and the kids being the passengers. When the parents are happy and aligned, the flight is pleasant, safe and reaches its destination.

When they're not, it gets turbulent and scary and who knows where they'll land.

Now on to another potential team challenge.

## BREAST FEEDING

The Center for Disease Control estimates that 76.9% of U.S. mothers breastfeed their infants immediately after birth, 47.2% do so for six months, and another 25.5% continue for twelve months. They don't have statistics past that time, but some moms continue for four or more years.

Doctors recommend exclusively breastfeeding for at least six months and, if doable, a year or more because it is Mother Nature's gold standard for healthy babies. Breast milk contains every vitamin and nutrient an infant needs in its first six months, offers lifelong protection against numerous illnesses, infections, and developing allergies. It reduces the risk of children, teens and adults becoming overweight, and dramatically lessens the danger of *sudden death syndrome (SIDS)*. Additionally, nursing diminishes mom's stress, postpartum depression, and defends against breast and ovarian cancer. So we know it's great for mother and child, but is it good for sex and relationship?

On the hopeful side, some women are eroticized by their infants sucking on their nipples and channel it into passion for their mates. Since nursing releases oxytocin that produces wonderful feelings of bonding and relaxation, mothers may also enjoy their bodies and thus be more interested in sex. Other moms don't find that breastfeeding either heightens or diminishes their libido.

Now for the more challenging aspects: for one thing, your mate's newly ample breasts can be tender, so you can look but maybe not touch. Her *prolactin*, the hormone that made her mammary glands bigger for nursing and stimulates her milk, is 20 times higher than pre-pregnancy. Although some breastfeeding women do have a menstrual cycle, prolactin inhibits ovulation for many—which is Nature's way of saying: "No more babies for now". E goes down after birth, but prolactin suppresses its production even further. That results in a drier vagina, hot flashes, and for many women, disinterest in sex. The fact that their testosterone is also low doesn't help their libidos either.

---

**NOTE**» *MOST MOMS FIND THEIR LIBIDO RETURNS WHEN THEY STOP BREASTFEEDING.*

---

There are women who nurse their kids for a long time, or wean one and have another baby and start nursing all over again. Meanwhile, their mates can get lonely, horny and hostile, and their relationships suffer. Moms often feel compassion for their mates and offer mercy sex, but they won't want to do it much if the sex hurts. The dads also might not enjoy it as well if they know their mates aren't really into it.

So, should women, especially those who are breast-feeding for a longer period of time, stop nursing so they can reconnect with their partners? It's a tough call if you're devoted to your baby's health but it's creating a bad situation at home. Before you decide it's an either/or situation, there are some key questions you need to answer.

## ALL WEATHER SOLUTIONS FOR MOTHERHOOD SEX

Whether or not a woman is breastfeeding, you have to go back to the basics to solve any sexual problems. There's nothing more fundamental than good, ongoing communication. What does your partner need? What do you need? Here's the Motherhood Sex Checklist to help you identify your issues. Then you can brainstorm on how, under the circumstances, to create the best conditions for mutually satisfying, loving sex.

# THE MOTHERHOOD SEX CHECKLIST

1. *Do you have good, honest communication?*

2. *Are you both willing to find mutually workable solutions?*

3. *Are you creating time to just enjoy being together?*

4. *Are you touching each other? Holding hands, hugging, kissing?*

5. *Are you creating time for sex?*

6. *Is she getting her period?*

7. *If she is, does she feel more sexual?*

8. *Is she breastfeeding?*

9. *Are her breasts sore?*

10. *Is she in pain? Why?*

11. *Is she going to a doctor to heal the problem?*

12. *Are you trying to have intercourse when she's dry?*

13. *Is she using lube? Estrogen cream?*

14. *Are you giving her enough foreplay?*

15. *Are you willing to have mutual oral sex or masturbation?*

16. *Is she exhausted?*

17. *Are you giving her all the help she's asking for?*

18. *Are you giving her "me-time"?*

19. *Is she neglecting herself?*

20. *Does she feel unattractive?*

21. *Are you supporting her in doing the feminine things that make her feel good?*

22. *Does she have the belief that the "baby comes first"?*

23. *Is she ignoring or minimizing your needs because of that idea?*

24. *Are you being a team?*

If the basics are covered, and your mate's E and T levels still leave her without a libido, do not despair. She can still want sex because you're being such a good partner and because she enjoys hugging, kissing and bonding. And many women discover that despite having no desire, they do get turned on once they're having sex. We'll end our pregnancy, postpartum and motherhood briefing and leave you to the joys of parenthood on that happy note.

## WHAT'S ON THE RADAR?

Next up for women: the end of fertility and the climate change it brings—peri and postmenopause. But first, the changes men experience from middle age on in *Andropause: Men's Climate Change.*

# CHAPTER FIVE

*The interesting thing about andropause is that men frequently don't recognize when they're going through it.*

## *ANDROPAUSE: MEN'S CLIMATE CHANGE*

In our experience, many men are oblivious to their own climate change; however their ever-observant, health-minded mates are supremely aware of it. In couples counseling and singularly, the ladies point out their men's lowered libido, fatigue, depression or irritability as signs that something is happening with his T. And they want it fixed because it's causing problems in their relationships. Of course males know when they're less interested in sex, are having trouble with their erections, are cranky or have less drive, but they often dismiss it as age, or worse, they blame their lover.

Even when men do check it out, they might not get much help because their doctors might not know much about it either. Why? Because despite being described in medical literature since the 1940s, physicians weren't even taught to recognize *andropause* until recently. It's a relatively new frontier and many doctors aren't trained to treat it or don't stay current with new developments. Consequently, andropause specialists agree that it's vastly under-diagnosed and under-treated.

## WHAT IS ANDROPAUSE?

It's referred to as "male menopause" because of the hormonal changes males often start experiencing in their early 50s—which is just about the time their mates might be exhibiting even more dramatic hormonal symptoms of their own.

Andropause is also called "man-o-pause" and 25 million American men are in it. Androgens, T being the principal one, are the male sex hormones that promote male charac-teristics. They don't actually pause as you age, but they can lower to a point where their balance to estrogen and proges-terone shifts so much that it causes problems. In 20%-30% of andropausal men, T declines to very low levels, causing a condition called *hypo* (low) *gonadism*, or *testosterone deficiency syndrome*, but we just call it *Low T*.

## CLIMATE CHANGING

Both men and women are destined to go through climate change; as their hormone levels and balances shift, distressing physical or emotional weather can result. Men's climate change is, however, very different from females. As you will read in *Menopause: Women's Climate Change,* your partner can have volatile swings in the quantity and ratio of her E and progesterone, which can suddenly cause nasty symptoms. You may have already witnessed some. Then her E and progesterone take a permanent nosedive, ensuring no more babies. Unfortunately, there's no guarantee that all her side effects will stop, too.

Andropause, on the other hand, just creeps up on you. It's a slow, stable process compared to women's sometimes stormy passage. After 30, your T goes down by 1%-2% a year. No big deal—until you're 55, when you have 25%-50% less. Not only that, but as your T declines, the proportion of your E increases. Young men have a ratio of 50:1 T to E. By the time you reach middle age, that ratio isn't what it used to be.

---

***NOTE*** *» AN AVERAGE 54-YEAR-OLD MAN HAS HIGHER ESTROGEN LEVELS THAN HIS 59-YEAR-OLD FEMALE COUNTERPART.*

---

What's going on? The answer might have a foreboding ring to it.

## ESTROGEN DOMINANCE

Don't worry, you'll always have more T than E. *Estrogen dominance* means you have too much estrogen in relation to the amount of testosterone and/or progesterone you are producing.

There's a joke about an airline pilot who made a rough, bumpy landing during a storm. Afterwards a rattled passenger nervously asked, "Did we land, or were we shot down?" Although we age slowly but surely, guys can still feel physically attacked when their hormonal balance tilts in favor of estrogen—especially with Low T.

Take a look at this checklist. Do you have any of these symptoms in greater or lesser degree? Or, ladies, does your lover?

## THE ANDROPAUSE/ESTROGEN DOMINANCE/LOW T CHECKLIST

- Lower sperm count

- Low sex drive or loss of libido

- Fewer spontaneous erections

- Difficulty in getting and maintaining erections

- Loss of muscle mass and tone

- Weight gain

- More body fat

- Male boobs

- Being bloated

- A slower immune system

- Fatigue

- Hot flashes

- Night sweats

- Problems sleeping

- Physical exhaustion

- Joint and muscle pain

- An enlarged prostate

---

**NOTE**» *STUDIES REVEAL MEN WITH THE HIGHEST LEVELS OF T HAVE THE LEAST PROSTATE ENLARGEMENT. MEN WITH THE HIGHEST LEVELS OF E HAVE THE MOST.*

---

Men's emotional and mental states can also suffer. You may be experiencing:

- Depression

- Anxiety

- Nervousness

- Mood swings

- Irritability

- Bad temper

- Less drive

- Less ambition

- A burnt out feeling

- Trouble concentrating

- Forgetfulness

## WHAT'S YOUR PERSONAL FORECAST?

Don't get too bummed about all the possible effects of andropause. Not everybody has the same symptoms or has them to the same degree; there's a range from mild to severe. If you have Low T, your symptoms could be on the more intense end of the scale.

There are a number of factors that determine how soon you might start experiencing andropause, but the most obvious are how much T you have to begin with and how fast it's diminishing. If you're a high-T guy whose T is declining at 1% a year, it could take awhile before you notice anything amiss. If you're average, 1% vs. 2% a year can make a big difference. If you start off with low levels to begin with, even 1% a year could trigger early symptoms.

Eventually, whatever your T-level is, you—and your partner—will probably confront at least a symptom or two. That's largely due to the happy fact that you will live long enough. In 1950, the average lifespan for men in the U.S.

was 65.5 years. Now it's 75 with the sunny prediction of more years ahead: according to the Congressional Research Service from the Library of Congress, males who live to 65 can generally expect to live an additional 16.2 years to 81.2. Congratulations.

Consequently you have more time for your T to naturally decrease and for your E to increase. You can, however, make estrogen dominance and Low T much worse by being overweight, drinking alcohol, using anabolic steroids, taking certain medicines and street drugs, and being constantly exposed to environmental toxins.

## BEING OVERWEIGHT

**❚❚** *One thing pilots have to do before every flight is check the weight of their plane. If it's too heavy, there might not be enough runway for it to get off the ground. Being overweight causes a lot of health issues that can ground you; one of them is having higher E levels because of aromatase, an enzyme in your fatty tissue.* **❚❚**

---

**NOTE**» *AROMATASE CONVERTS TESTOSTERONE TO ESTROGEN.*

---

You read it right. While you're busy chowing down those extra carbs, aromatase is busy turning your T into estrogen. It's particularly active in your belly fat.

If you're obese and have Low T, you might find yourself stuck in a vicious loop: Low T creates more belly fat, upping the aromatase activity, which in turn converts more T into E. Now the T is even lower and creates more abdominal fat, which further ups the aromatase activity, etc.

---

**NOTE**» *ACCORDING TO THE CENTERS FOR DISEASE CONTROL AND PREVENTION, 32.2% OF AMERICAN MEN ARE OBESE AND AN ADDITIONAL 40.1% ARE OVERWEIGHT.*

---

About two-thirds of both U.S. adult males and females are overweight or obese but surveys reveal that the majority of them think their weight is normal. Maybe it's because they look around and see most people look like them. But being in denial doesn't change the facts: the more overweight you are, the less testosterone, the more estrogen, and the more loss of man power.

❚❚*I'm 15 pounds overweight, so I know how hard it is to get rid of visceral belly fat. I've been told to be sure to do weight bearing exercise to keep the testosterone high, which I do. But cardio and diet are also required. Serious discipline is needed to get rid of that big E-generating belly.* ❚❚

The results of the Diabetes Prevention Program study offer stunning proof that lifestyle changes work. Researchers evaluated 891 overweight, prediabetic men with an average age of 54 to see if they could delay or avoid the disease through weight loss. Since Low T is prevalent in overweight men, they also studied T levels.

The men were divided into three groups: 293 men reduced fat and calorie intake and did 150 minutes of exercise a week; 305 took the diabetes drug metformin; and 293 received a placebo. After one year, the men in the lifestyle group lost an average of 17 pounds and had a 15% increase in their T levels.

---

**NOTE**» *THERE WAS ALSO A 46% DECREASE*
*IN HOW MANY OF THEM HAD LOW T.*

---

There were no significant changes in T levels in the other two groups. The lifestyle warriors also reduced their risk of progressing to diabetes.

So, with this encouraging proof in mind, diet and exercise on!

## ALCOHOL

❚❚*Being 30-plus years sober, I'm also familiar with all the downsides of being an alcoholic. Aside from making you sick and ruining your life, it makes you fatter, boosting your fat cells' conversion of testosterone into estrogen. At the same time, it's the liver's responsibility to get rid of excess estrogen, and alcohol can prevent it from doing its job.* ❚❚

## ANABOLIC STEROIDS

If you want to be a senior muscle man, using anabolic steroids is a terrible idea. They shut down T production and elevate E production, and can produce the harsh andropausal symptoms of "male boobs," reduced sperm count, enlarged prostate and impotence. Younger men might be able to reverse them if they stop, but you're already vulnerable. No more needs to be said.

## HIGH-PRESSURE ZONE

Do you live in a high-pressure zone? Are you always stressed out? Does your job, finances, kids, relationship, not having a relationship, not having enough time, the morning drive or any of a million other daily pressures make you chronically anxious? Does just reading this list raise your blood pressure?

If so, you're running on cortisol, the stress hormone. How does that affect estrogen dominance? Progesterone is the precursor to both your cortisol and your testosterone. When you're highly stressed or live in a state of chronic stress, your body goes into "fight or flight" mode. Survival is its #1 priority, so your body converts more progesterone to cortisol and lowers its testosterone production.

To make matters worse, some progesterone is produced in your adrenals, and being continually stressed out can cause adrenal fatigue. That means they produce less progesterone to convert to T to begin with.

## ILL WINDS

We're responsible for what and how much we eat and drink, abuse steroids, or live in stress. Maybe what we've done has made us sick or maybe we've got bad genes or were exposed to toxins. Whatever the cause, there are some illnesses that generate estrogen.

Liver diseases raise estrogen levels because they impede the liver's ability to eliminate toxins, including excess estrogen. Some adrenal, liver, lung, pituitary, and testes tumors also increase the amount of E.

## MEDICATIONS

There are a lot of commonly used medications that contain or produce E. Taking anti-fungals or antibiotics such as ampicillin or tetracycline for a few weeks shouldn't be much of a problem. But if you're on antidepressants that raise aromatase, or ulcer medication for the long run, you might want to check how they're affecting your estrogen levels. Drugs that lower cholesterol, like statins, and some medicines that lower glucose also affect T levels.

## HAZARDOUS MATERIALS

**❚❚** *When I was flying in Vietnam, the jungle vegetation was so thick we couldn't see the Vietcong, so pilots sprayed millions of gallons of the herbicidal mix called "Agent Orange" to defoliate it. A lot of Vietnam vets and the Vietnamese who were exposed to it now suffer from its side effects, which include various cancers and other vicious diseases, and birth defects in their children.*

**❚❚** *While Agent Orange produced horrifying effects on a large, but limited number of people, the widespread use of chemicals in modern society has more subtle and far-reaching consequences.* **❚❚**

One problem that you may not know about is that many chemicals are *estrogenic,* meaning they have the same or similar characteristics as estrogen and therefore act like it.

Great. The last thing you need is more E, but you ingest, inhale and absorb a constant drizzle of estrogenic chemicals through your skin. The long-range forecast is that the E builds up in your body and it's hard for your liver to detoxify it.

## THE ESTROGENIC CHECKLIST

What's estrogenic? It's more like what isn't? Take a look:

- Pesticides sprayed on our fruits and vegetables
- Herbicides

- Food additives

- Commercially raised, steroid-fed poultry, meat, and pork

- Plastics that leach into our food, water and beverages from plastic wrap, can linings and food containers

- Soaps, detergent and household cleaning products

- Skin care products

- Air fresheners and perfumes and all artificial scents

- Paints, lacquers and solvents

- Car exhaust and indoor toxins

- Industrial wastes

See what we mean? Estrogen-mimicking products are everywhere. Now before you do the guy thing and discount this info, keep in mind the negative impact your andropausal symptoms have on you and on your relationship. And even if you can't eliminate everything that's estrogenic, you can reduce them with a little effort. To learn how read the *Reducing Environmental Estrogens* checklist in Appendix 1.

---

***NOTE***» *LADIES, THESE CHECKLISTS ARE ALSO VITAL TO YOUR HEALTH. TOO MUCH E FEEDS CERTAIN TUMORS AND IMPACTS OTHER FEMALE HEALTH ISSUES.*

---

## WEATHER ALERTS

You might want to add "through andropause and menopause" to the "through sickness and health" vow of committed couples. You and your partner's "change of life" can physically and emotionally alter both of you in unexpected ways. It's not optional to ignore harmful symptoms that hurt your relationship. Therefore, you need to talk to each other about what's going on and figure out how to handle this new weather together. With that goal in mind, let's look at...

## THE GRUMPY OLD MAN SYNDROME

**You know you're in andropause when everyone around you has an attitude problem.**

Who likes a grump? No one, especially mates. A lot of men complain about their lovers' PMS moods and perimeno-pausal mood swings. Now some poor unlucky women get to see what they are like. Andropausal men can become chroni-cally hypersensitive, angry, frustrated and irritable. In recent years it's been given a clinical name, so it's official: *IMS* or *Irritable Male Syndrome*. It can also be related with stress and a feeling of loss of male identity. That's no fun for anyone and is a source of conflict with older couples.

## SEX

**Did you hear about the recent sex survey? It showed that 90% of 20-year-old men have sex four times a**

**week and that by the time they reach 40 they are still capable of telling the same pathetic lie.**

Needless to say, sex is vitally important to men. So much of their self-image and manly pride are connected to the sexual pleasure, intimacy and the release that males give to and get from their lovers—and in those solo times, themselves.

As T declines, so does the frequency with which men think about and want sex. A lot of guys have told us that not being obsessed by sex all the time is a relief because it was so distracting. They're still having good, though less frequent, sex and feel fine about it. They just accept it as part of life and adjust to the changes as they age.

Men do get upset, however, when they lose their desire or when they can't rely on getting hard or staying hard long enough to orgasm. It can also be distressing to their mates. Why? For two reasons: first, these women still need sex; second, their men get so frustrated /angry/ depressed that they create scenes in the bedroom and alienation in the home.

## TROUBLING WEATHER

**Don't worry about avoiding temptation—as you grow older, it starts avoiding you.**

Menopausal women can suddenly lose interest in sex, have problems climaxing, or get so dry it's too painful to have it. Plenty of men have come to counseling bemoaning this fact and some consider getting divorced or having affairs. If women replace their diminishing E, progesterone, and testosterone, their sexual issues get handled, but they might be afraid of side effects. Much more on that in *Weather Protection for Women* in Appendix 2.

When females do choose hormone replacement or don't have any negative sexual symptoms to begin with, they too, need partners who satisfy them.

---

**NOTE**» *WORLDWIDE, A SIGNIFICANT NUMBER OF WOMEN AGED 50 AND OVER STATE THAT THE MAJOR REASON THEY ARE DEPRESSED IS THEIR LOVERS' LOW LIBIDOS AND/OR IMPOTENCE.*

---

Aside from the physical issues, a depressed or irritable man with self-confidence and motivation issues isn't usually the profile of an active, interested lover.

We're finding more and more frustrated women initiating couples counseling to address sex. It's blatantly clear to them that they need help in navigating past both their lovers' resistance to dealing with their sexual problems, and their own growing hostility. Younger women are particularly frantic when their older husbands leave them hot and wanting.

In general, there are some basic relationship problems to deal with in couple's counseling, and the same is true when the focus is solving sexual issues. It could be that stress, resentments, invalidation of each other's reality, and / or horrible communication are destroying any desire for one or both to get intimate. Therefore, getting the communication going, fixing it and creating understanding are always the first steps in solving anything. Then couples are motivated to act.

In regards to sex, men generally need to do a number of things, starting with having their T and other hormones checked out and possibly corrected with Testosterone Replacement Therapy (TRT) and lifestyle changes. Whatever the hormone situation turns out to be, couples still need to acknowledge age and how to realistically modify their lovemaking so a good time is had by all.

If you can do this without counseling, even better. Yes, low sex drive and sexual reliability are touchy subjects, but hey, as you get older they can happen.

Since andropause is a slow but sure decline, keeping your partner in the loop should be standard operating procedure. If it isn't, she might assume you are steadily losing interest in her, which is painful. Predict rain and thunderstorms. Even if you're not good at talking about and dealing with difficult emotional issues, your mate probably can do it in her sleep. So, be proactive: communicate, then do what you need to do.

## LIFESTYLE CHANGES

You're a few paragraphs away from a briefing on how to check your T levels and Testosterone Replacement Therapy. Whether it turns out that you're a candidate for TRT or not, you'll probably need to make some lifestyle changes. What are they? For starters, taking responsibility for any of things we detailed that make your symptoms worse. On the proactive side that would mean eating better, exercising and losing weight, drinking moderately, eliminating anabolic steroids, changing your attitude and your life so you don't live in a state of stress, and cutting down on your exposure to environmental toxins. Also see if you can change prescriptions that raise your E or lower your T. Making these alterations might seem overwhelming, but a positive, can-do attitude goes a long way. A man on a mission to improve his health, one step at a time, can thrive during climate change.

## *HOT AND STEAMY*

Lucky for us and for our lovers, modern medicine has good news for aging men: Cialis, Viagra and Levitra, so there's no need to go without. If you're having sexual issues, you can still enjoy sizzling sex the good old-fashioned way. Now might also be a great time for you and your mate to expand and explore new ways to make love. Dare we say it? You can learn to be an even better lover than you were when you were younger. You can find out what she likes, take more time in foreplay, fantasize and role play, or learn some new techniques. The main thing is to be a team, be compassionate with each other, and mutually figure out what you need to do to satisfy each other.

## WARM AND BALMY

Being a more mature lover can also give you the gift of finding more satisfaction through deeper intimacy. Aging men have an advantage. As we mentioned in *Oxytocin: Love In The Sun*, without all your T blocking this bonding hormone, you can enjoy the warm, balmy weather your woman always did—cuddling, kissing, and holding each other. The closeness you feel might be a revelation; this is the kind of connection she's always wanted with you.

## BEING SINGLE

❚❚*If you are dating, you also have the benefit of not being driven by your T to jump into the sack with the wrong woman just because she's available. Right up to my 40s and early 50s I was somewhat indiscriminate about who I had sex with. I wasn't aware that my testosterone was decreasing or that my oxytocin was increasing, but I did notice a change. I started becoming a lot choosier and more careful. Even though I still looked at every woman I passed and wanted to have a lot of sex, I didn't feel the urgency to rush into it. I began to look more for someone I could relate to and could talk to about my interests and who would share her interests with me. I also became more conscious of what a woman's energy was like and wanted to be sure I wanted that energy mingling with mine. ❚❚*

This kind of discernment leads to better, more intimate relationships and better, more satisfying sex.

If you're single and have sexual issues, don't be discouraged about reaching out and dating. Please don't let feeling embarrassed or vulnerable stop you from being with a loving partner. The key to a happy relationship is finding the woman who meets your needs and whose needs you meet. Desire, libido, frequency, and the kind of sex that is enjoyed vary from person to person—whether or not they're in climate change. Plus, there are many peri and postmenopausal women who have their own sexual issues, such as diminished or no desire, or a dry vagina that makes intercourse painful. Most women climax from clitoral stimulation, so getting or maintaining a hard-on isn't even necessary to satisfy them. Moreover, sex is only part of the equation: companionship, support and love also matter. Be honest, communicate with your prospects and see if there's a match. If not, keep looking and connecting.

And of course, do all the things that will make you a better lover, including making lifestyle changes and getting your hormone levels tested to see if you have Low T or other medical issues that are impacting you sexually. On that note, here's the TRT briefing.

## TRACKING YOUR WEATHER

*"Everybody complains about the weather, but nobody does anything about it." Mark Twain*

Except that was before hormonal blood and saliva tests. Nowadays you can go to a doctor and get a *Male Hormone Test Panel* to check on your T, progesterone and E levels. Take a look at the panel in *Appendix 1*. It includes a few other important hormones we haven't mentioned that affect andropause or cause some of the same symptoms as Low T or estrogen dominance.

We're giving you all this data so you can be an informed patient and select the right doctor. As mentioned earlier, not all physicians are created equal in their understanding of andropause or Low T. A 1996 article in the FDA Consumer Magazine estimated that only 5% of Low T men were being treated for it. Additionally, a 2008 three-year observational study found 88% of their Low T subjects also weren't getting treatment from their physicians. You could be one of those guys.

The wrong practitioner will just test for your T levels, and if they're in normal range send you away untreated; or give you something like a sleeping pill or an anti-depressant, which might address the symptoms, but not the core issues or the imbalance itself. We know because some of our andropausal clients tell us they were tested and their T was "normal," yet they still have the same problems.

So here's some more important information: as you recall, T is highest in the mornings, in the winter, and in the fall, and frequently varies from week to week. Therefore the tests have to be taken before 10 A.M. and no less than twice, with at least a week intervening. Illness, stress and some medications can also affect results.

---

**NOTE**» ONE STUDY THAT TRACKED UNTREATED LOW T MEN OVER 15 YEARS FOUND THAT 50% OF THEM HAD NORMAL T LEVELS IN SOME OF THEIR ONGOING TESTS.

---

Then there's the controversy about which are the best tests, how accurately they measure T-levels and what actually is "normal." Currently, there is no accepted standard for measuring Low T because different labs have different cut-off ranges for designating it.

---

**NOTE**» THE FDA RECOMMENDS 300 NG/DL TOTAL T AS THE STANDARD FOR LOW T.

---

*Total testosterone* measures both the 96%-99% of T in the blood that is bound to a protein and the 1%-4% that is not bound *("free testosterone")*.

But what if your test for total T indicates you're in the normal range and you still feel crappy? It could mean you should have also been tested for free T. Since only free testosterone circulates in your bloodstream and is available for your body to use, it needs to be replaced if its levels are low—even if your total T is normal. Get both tests.

All these question marks surrounding the tests give your doctor some discretion in weighing your lab results against your symptoms and determining if you have Low T. Even if you don't, he or she can evaluate the strength of your estrogen dominance or see what else could be causing your symptoms. Hopefully your primary care physician is an andropause expert, but if not, your best bet is to go to someone who specializes in treating men's hormonal deficiencies, excesses and imbalances. Recruit your partner to help you find one; women tend to be interested in health and good at asking questions.

---

**WARNING**» *DO NOT SELF-DIAGNOSE AND SELF-PRESCRIBE!*

---

You don't want to *be* the wrong doctor, and give yourself the wrong diagnosis or a random dosage of some over-the-counter or Internet remedy.

## GOT TESTOSTERONE?

*The U.S. Food and Drug Administration (FDA)* only approves *Testosterone Replacement Therapy (TRT)* for men with Low T levels who also suffer from associated medical conditions, such as: a failure of the testicles to make T due to genetic problems, trauma or chemotherapy or testicles which have not descended into the scrotum.

On the other hand, the U.S. Endocrine Society's Clinical Guidelines expand the use of T supplementation to symptomatic, Low T men in order "to improve their sexual function, sense of well-being, muscle mass and strength, and bone mineral density." In practice, doctors generally adhere to these broader standards.

---

**NOTE**» *LIKE MEDICATIONS FOR OTHER CHRONIC CONDITIONS, TRT IS USUALLY PRESCRIBED FOR LIFE.*

---

There is a variety of ways to take it: in a gel (the most popular form), cream, skin patch, mouth patch, lozenge, by injection, or by pellets that are implanted. All these formulations go directly into the blood stream, thus bypassing the liver. Pills, on the other hand, go through the liver and are rarely prescribed because they are ineffective and may increase liver toxicity or the risk of liver cancer. Another choice you may want to consider is whether the formula is synthetic or *bioidentical*. (Bioidentical means the hormones are identical, on a molecular level, with the hormones in your body).

*(Go to Testosterone Replacement Options in Appendix 1 to see the pros and cons of each formulation.)*

## CAN I USE THESE FORMULATIONS IF MY T LEVELS REALLY ARE NORMAL?

Although we've been cautioning against doctors who don't understand or treat Low T, paradoxically, at the other end of the spectrum, are doctors who cheerfully dispense T to men with normal levels.

---

*WARNING» UP TO 25% OF PRESCRIPTIONS
ARE NOW WRITTEN WITHOUT EVEN
MEASURING HORMONE LEVELS!*

---

Confirming this point is the 2000–2011 joint study between the United States and the United Kingdom to see how many men were testing for Low T and using TRT. Two unexpected findings were that a large number of U.S. men had initiated TRT without recent testing or had normal T levels.

Some critics attribute the overprescription of TRT to the aggressive "Is It Low-T?" awareness campaign. Since Abbot Laboratories, the manufacturer of AndroGel, initiated it in 2008, T sales have risen 1800% to more than $1.9 billion in 2012. In all fairness, however, many of these sales could be to men who really need it and it's up to doctors to prescribe it properly.

But why not supplement your T if your levels are normal and you want to get that T-high or perform better athletically? Because of potentially harmful side effects, like maybe losing your own natural ability to make T yourself.

---

*WARNING» YOUR BRAIN SIGNALS YOUR
TESTES TO MAKE THE RIGHT AMOUNT OF
T. IF YOUR LEVELS ARE NORMAL AND YOU
SUPPLEMENT THE T, YOUR BRAIN REGISTERS
YOU HAVE MORE THAN ENOUGH AND STOPS
SIGNALING YOUR TESTES TO MAKE MORE,
SO THE CELLS THAT PRODUCE T BECOME
SUPPRESSED. AS A RESULT, YOUR T LEVELS
FALL.*

---

Thus, if you use TRT when your T levels are normal, your body may not be able to resume the same level of T production if you decide to stop.

Another potent consequence could be the effect T might have on your sperm.

---

**CAUTION**» *IF YOU'RE OLDER AND GREYER, BUT STILL WANT KIDS, THERE'S A CHANCE TRT COULD REDUCE YOUR SPERM COUNT AND MAKE YOU INFERTILE. ALSO IF YOU'RE 50+, YOUR SPERM COULD BE DAMAGED.*

---

Those chilling possibilities aside, the lack of studies or trials on the effects of TRT on men with normal levels means you don't have a clue as to what else might turn out to be a problem.

## SUNNY FORECAST—TRT BENEFITS

T is the sex hormone, and most health care professionals, Low T men and studies have found that replacing it consistently improves:

- Sex drive

- Arousal

- The frequency of spontaneous erections

- Erectile function

Some athletes and body builders are seduced into using steroids, even with their chilling side effects, because they:

202

- Increase muscles mass and/or

- Decrease fat mass

- Increase strength in some muscle groups

    Other reported, but less consistent, benefits are:

- Increased bone density

- Increased energy

- Improved mood

- Decreased depression

- Improved cognitive function

## *VARYING WEATHER PROTECTION*

There's a lot of variation amongst men as to which symptoms and to what degree TRT helps. This is due to the endlessly repeated fact that everyone is different and that older men might have illnesses and use medications that affect both their T production and their TRT treatment. Hence some men might be thrilled about the results, while others might hardly notice them or be anywhere in between. Generally though, the response is positive.

Since andropause hasn't been a hot area of interest until recently, there's a lot of catching up to do. TRT studies have ranged from a month to three years. So far, there are no large-scale, placebo-controlled studies on its long-term effects. There are also no standards, so researchers are using different applications, dosages, populations, and numbers of men. Thus they're coming up with different risk/benefits results.

Ditto for practitioners, who are also using different formulations and doses. In addition, they monitor their patients' levels to determine what amount they need to keep them in the mid-range of the T scale. The question is "what is mid-scale"? Since there isn't a definitive standard, it can be anywhere from 350 ng/dL to 700 ng/dL. However, 600ng/dl might turn out to be the magic number: recent findings show 400 ng/dL increased night time erections, 500 ng/dL increased frequency of sexual intercourse, and 600 ng/dL increased sexual desire.

Another thing to be aware of is that, depending on what condition is being treated, TRT usually takes anywhere from three weeks to six months to work. Keeping in mind all these different variables and the relative dearth of research, let's look at ...

## WEATHER PROTECTION RISKS

Does having Low T and andropausal symptoms automatically make you a candidate for TRT? No. TRT can worsen a few health conditions, thus tests are in order before the "all clear" is given to use it. Thorough prostate screening, rectal exam and PSA tests are vital.

---

***WARNING*»** *RESEARCH HAS SHOWN THAT T STIMULATES THE GROWTH OF PROSTATE AND MALE BREAST TUMORS.*

---

One man in six has prostate cancer, with aging men the most susceptible, so the test can potentially eliminate a lot of men (and save a lot of lives). See the *Male Hormone Test Panel* in the Appendix 1 for other required tests.

---

***NOTE*»** *ON THE POSITIVE SIDE, THERE'S NO EVIDENCE THAT TRT INCREASES THE RISK OF PROSTATE CANCER IN MEN WHO DON'T ALREADY HAVE IT.*

---

Doctors are also on the lookout for other conditions that TRT can have a detrimental effect on, such as:

- Severe congestive heart failure

- Difficulty urinating due to a larger prostate that squeezes the tube carrying the urine

- A severely blocked urine flow, which can back up and hurt one or both kidneys

- A high red blood cell count: TRT increases red blood cell count, which could thicken the blood and increase the possibility of it clotting

- Sleep apnea—TRT can sometimes affect the central breathing control and exacerbate sleep apnea

## THE WEATHER PROTECTION DEBATE

Since Low T levels in men has been associated with higher mortality, researchers have been eager to see if supplementing with T helps prolong life. The results, as we mentioned earlier, are conflicting: multiple studies show that TRT protects against heart disease and decreases mortality and others find it can increase illness and death.

On the pro side, a 2007 study followed 794 men aged 50-91 for over eleven years. They discovered that the men with T levels in the lowest quarter were 40% more likely to die than the men in the highest group. Low T also increased the risk of heart attack.

In another study, researchers assessed 1031 Low T male veterans, aged 40 and older, with no history of prostate cancer. After five years the 398 men who received TRT had a 39% decreased mortality rate compared to the men who didn't.

On the con side, there are a few studies of older men with some preexisting conditions that are causing concern. One is a 2005-2011 observational study in the U.S. Veteran Affairs health system. The researchers followed 8709 men, whose average age was 60 when they entered the study, had Low T and were undergoing imaging of the blood vessels of their heart to watch for coronary artery disease. There were 1223 veterans who began TRT, with 20% of them having a history of strokes, 50% suffering from diabetes and more than 80% having coronary artery disease.

---

**NOTE**» *AFTER THREE YEARS, THERE WAS A 29% INCREASED RISK OF STOKE, HEART ATTACK AND DEATH IN THE GROUP THAT USED TRT.*

---

Then there's the Testosterone in Older Men with Mobility Limitations observational study of 209 Low T men, whose average age was 74; it was stopped early because 23 subjects in the TRT group had heart attacks while only five in the placebo group did. Again, there was a high prevalence of underlying conditions–obesity, hypertension, diabetes, and high cholesterol and high triglycerides that can lead to heart attacks.

Are you sufficiently confused? Are you wondering how all this applies to you? So is the FDA, which is currently evaluating the increased risk of stroke, heart attack and death in men taking TRT.

At the same time, some answers might be on the way, at least for men 65 and older who have Low T. The National Institute of Health (NIH) has launched the clinical research T Trial of 800 seniors who will use either a T gel or a placebo for one year. The aim is to determine if TRT "will help their walking, vitality, sexual function, memory, blood count, and cardiovascular risk."

Stand by.

## WHAT IF YOU DON'T HAVE ANY HEALTH ISSUES TO PREVENT YOU FROM TAKING TRT?

The risks are usually pretty mild. The most frequent are rashes, itching, or irritation on the place where you applied the T. Other potential side effects are oily skin acne, mildly decreased urination, mild fluid retention, and breast enlargement. On the emotional front, you could also become irritable and act aggressively.

Again, there isn't conclusive research on which preparations and doses produce these adverse reactions and who's most likely to get them.

Like any medication, you need to decide if the benefits of TRT outweigh its risks. A "yes" answer could improve your quality of life, but you need to check with your doctor every three to six months to make sure your symptoms are improving and you're not getting any adverse reactions. Based on the results, you may need to try a different application or dose.

## ADAPTING TO CLIMATE CHANGE

There's still a lot to learn about andropause, but at least there's a growing body of information and tools to help you adapt to it. And age is what you make it.

**ll** *I've found that once you face the facts and get on track taking care of yourself, you can use what you know and make your life as rich or richer than ever. Okay, so there* *are physical things you can't do as well anymore, but there are things you can do better, particularly in terms of being a better mate. //*

Which brings us to your next big relationship challenge: understanding and supporting your partner through her own potentially turbulent change of life. You'll learn what weather to expect and get some helpful strategies for dealing with it in Menopause: Women's Climate Change.

Meanwhile, the Air Quality Index is good today, so go ahead—breathe every chance you get.

# CHAPTER SIX

*While male's climate change is slow and steady, women's is erratic and unpredictable.*

## MENOPAUSE: WOMEN'S CLIMATE CHANGE

Female hormones don't have that regular, orderly march down to lower levels, like men's testosterone; theirs ebb and flow for years and bottom out when they finally reach their "change of life". And during those years approaching menopause, which way the wind will blow can be anyone's guess.

### WHAT'S GOING ON?

Menopause is all about ovaries and the cessation of their two basic baby-making jobs. To review: 1) Ovaries are a woman's sex hormone factory, producing the estrogen and progesterone that fuel her brain and body and regulate her monthly cycles so she can get pregnant. They also make the testosterone that stokes her sex drive and gives her energy. 2) They create eggs.

## THE DEFINING MOMENT

*Menopause* is the day 12 months after a woman stops getting her period, forever. That's it. Her climate is officially and irrevocably altered: no more eggs; minimal ovarian output of sex hormones.

What leads up to the day her menses stands still is *perimenopause,* the unstable two to ten years leading up to menopause. That's when her ovaries are slowing down and her estrogen and progesterone production is becoming completely unpredictable, confusing her and you. The ultimate trajectory is, of course, down.

*Postmenopause* is what happens for the rest of her life. The average age for menopause is 51.

---

**NOTE**» *A WOMAN PRODUCES THE SAME AMOUNT OF ESTROGEN AND PROGESTERONE AFTER MENOPAUSE AS SHE DID BEFORE PUBERTY.*

---

Can you imagine producing the same amount of T you did pre-puberty? That would be a big change, buddy. Expect some adjustments in the woman you love.

# THE WONDER YEARS

Perimenopause could be called "the wonder years" because you're both wondering what the hell is happening. This transitional time in a woman's life usually starts in her 40s but can begin as early as her late 30s or after her mid-50s. As pointed out, it can last anywhere from two to ten years. Can we get a little more vague?

---

**NOTE**» PERIMENOPAUSE CAN START A FEW YEARS EARLIER IN SMOKERS THAN IN NON-SMOKERS.

---

What makes it all the more confusing is that during those years, whenever they happen to start and end on your specific woman, she can also:

- Get her period, with the attendant hormonal ups and downs

- Get pregnant

- Yo-yo through perimenopause

It's challenging to forecast the weather when these hormonal possibilities happen simultaneously. Plus, since there's no common flight plan, start or arrival time, the symptoms can come and go and vary in type and intensity, and women can get confused and misidentify what's happening to them. They may wonder: Why am I so emotional? Is it my menstrual cycle? Stress? Am I having a mid-life crisis? Am I sick? Is it menopause? Or in a worst-case scenario, are YOU the problem?

## HOW CAN YOU TELL WHEN PERIMENOPAUSE IS STARTING?

Your lover needs to look for slight variations in her menstrual cycle. If she normally menstruates every 28 days, she might find she's getting her period sooner or later than usual and her flow can get a little lighter or heavier. As time goes by, these deviations from the norm become more dramatic. Her flow can get much lighter or heavier, and her periods can become more erratic: the days between them can be much shorter or longer; she can completely skip one or more for months at a time, even for eleven months, but then it starts again.

---

*NOTE» THE AVERAGE AGE WHEN IRREGULAR CYCLES START IS 47.*

---

## PREGNANCY DURING PERIMENOPAUSE

---

*WARNING» SINCE IT CAN BE HARD TO PREDICT A WOMAN'S CYCLE, YOU NEED TO BE EXTRA CAREFUL TO PREVENT AN UNWANTED PREGNANCY.*

---

You both might assume that your lover is too old to conceive, but you could get a perimenopause surprise. To be safe, use condoms or any type of birth control that she feels comfortable with.

On the other hand, you might want to conceive and be part of the growing trend to have kids after 40. In both these situations, the rhythm method, as described in *Estrogen: Women's Weather,* comes in handy to predict when your lover is fertile.

## CAN ANYTHING PRECIPITATE CLIMATE CHANGE?

Yes.

## EARLY CLIMATE CHANGE

A pre-existing condition such as an autoimmune disease, chronic stress, or too much athletic training, can mess up a woman's ovarian function. So can chemotherapy and radiation treatment for cancer, and hysterectomies in which the woman keeps at least one ovary. When any of these events happen, your partner can become that one in a hundred woman who reaches menopause in her 30s or early 40s.

---

**NOTE**» *30% OF WOMEN WHO GO THROUGH PREMATURE MENOPAUSE ARE GENETICALLY DISPOSED TO IT.*

---

Early climate change happens faster, usually in one to three years, and has more and harsher symptoms. Also, because women need estrogen to build bones and for heart health, postmenopausal women have a higher risk for *osteoporosis* (thin, brittle, breakable bones) and heart attacks. Those dangers increase with premature menopause because there are so many more years of low estrogen production.

What to do? Fortunately, doctors usually prescribe replacing estrogen and progesterone to ease the onslaught of symptoms and to help prevent the illnesses. Our *Weather Protection For Women* section in Appendix 2 discusses *Hormone Replacement Therapy (HRT)* and *Bioidentical Hormone Therapy (BHRT)* in detail. Bioidentical hormones have exactly the same chemical and molecular structures that a woman naturally produces. The HRT hormones do not.

## ABRUPT CLIMATE CHANGE

This worst-case scenario is a result of medical intervention and, unfortunately, about 25% of American women experience it. Having a hysterectomy where both ovaries are removed is a major cause. Another is using drugs that shrink uterine fibroids that instantly stop their egg production and periods. Chemotherapy or radiation can also cause sudden menopause.

This is a hurricane a woman's body isn't prepared for. One minute she can ovulate, the next she can't. Even though perimenopause can be very difficult for some women, at least their bodies are undergoing a process and have time to adjust. In artificial menopause, the precipitous drop in hormones can cause brutal symptoms. The standard treatment is immediate hormone replacement therapy to ease them.

Now that we've got the basics covered, we're ready for the nitty-gritty—how the symptoms of climate change can play out in the way your mate feels and acts.

## FREAKISH WEATHER

**Q: What can a man do while his wife is going through perimenopause?**
**A: Keep busy. If you're handy with tools, you can finish the basement. When you are done you will have a place to live.**

The truth behind the joke is that your lover's "change of life" can be a demanding time for her and for you. She could be wrestling with various degrees of physical, mental or emotional distress. You might not know what's going on, you might be trying to cope, or you might feel powerless because you don't know what to do to fix her. Sound familiar? Yes, it's another phase in a woman's life cycle that makes male/female relationships so challenging.

## WHAT ARE THE SYMPTOMS?

Remember your woman's PMS symptoms? What we're looking at here can be much more dramatic. An inspired cartoon by "Danc" illustrates the Seven Dwarfs of Perimenopause: Itchy, Bitchy, Sweaty, Bloaty, Sleepy, Forgetful, and Psycho.

Better to laugh than to cry, right?

It isn't just having less estrogen or progesterone that causes troublesome symptoms. There's also how the hormones balance. Remember estrogen dominance from the *Andropause: Male Climate Change* chapter? That's too much estrogen in relation to progesterone. When it happens in female climate change, your lover can experience:

- Bloating

- Tender, swelling breasts

- Emotional problems: depression, hostility, irritability and mood swings

- Weight gain

- Decreased desire for sex

On the other hand, too little estrogen can cause:

- Hot flashes

- Night sweats

- Problems sleeping

- Mood swings

- The same depression, hostility and irritability that too much E causes

- Anxiety

- A variety of cognitive problems, fuzzy brain and memory lapses

- Dry skin, vaginal dryness, vaginal itchiness or burning

- Thinning of her vaginal wall

- Painful intercourse as a result of the last two points

- A diminished sexual response and diminished sexual pleasure

- Vaginal or bladder infections

- Incontinence and urinary tract infections

- Migraines

## WHY ARE THERE SO MANY DIFFERENT SYMPTOMS?

Estrogen is the power fuel that keeps your lover's brain healthy and ensures its proper functioning. So, it directly or indirectly affects every brain cell, which in turn affects her whole body. Plus, there are E receptors in all her organs, including her heart, skin and bones. There are also progesterone and T receptors throughout her brain and body. When her hormones decline and go out of balance, her body goes into emergency mode as it tries to rectify and acclimatize to all the changes.

## DO ALL WOMEN HAVE ALL THESE SYMPTOMS?

No, some lucky 10%-20% just breeze through with nary a weather event. Others experience mild disturbances and others encounter severe storms. Not everyone has the same symptoms or combination of symptoms.

---

*NOTE» WOMEN WHO SUFFERED PMS OR POSTPARTUM SYMPTOMS ARE MORE SENSITIVE TO DROPS IN ESTROGEN AND ARE MORE LIKELY TO HAVE THEM IN PERIMENOPAUSE.*

---

With that in mind, let's look at the most common ones.

## GLOBAL WARMING

**"I'm not having a hot flash. I'm having a power surge."**

The one positive effect of perimenopause on your relationship is that there are no gender–related "it's hot" vs. "it's cold" arguments. You're both hot.

As menopause approaches, approximately 75%-85% of women get hot flashes. There's a sudden rush of heat on their upper bodies and their faces, which redden. Most ladies have mild to moderate hot flashes that last 30 seconds to 10 minutes. But some can experience them for up to an hour, and can get boiling hot.

---

*NOTE» 10%-15% OF WOMEN HAVE TO GO TO THE DOCTOR DUE TO SEVERE HOT FLASHES.*

---

Your lover's power surge is followed by "Sweaty". Now she's perspiring— a little, or a downpour. A chill can follow.

When it happens when she's asleep, she can wake up soaking wet from "night sweats." More on that in a minute.

## WHY THE HEATWAVE?

Your woman's declining estrogen is the culprit. There is a cause and effect relationship between estrogen and the *hypothalamus*, he part of our brain nicknamed the 'body's thermostat" because one of its jobs is to control our temperature. When estrogen drops, it registers as "too hot" and sends out a red alert: her heart instantly pumps more rapidly, and the blood vessels in her skin dilate to increase her blood flow and radiate the heat off her body. At the same time her sweat glands are doing their part to cool her off by perspiring. The hotter she gets, the cooler she needs to get—hence the potential for "flash floods".

---

*NOTE» HER HEART CAN BEAT SCARY FAST DURING A SEVERE HOT FLASH, BUT IT'S NOT A HEALTH RISK.*

---

Aside from a rapidly beating heart and heavy perspiration, women can also become dizzy, nauseated, weak and anxious, and suffer headaches or problems breathing before or during a flash.

Even when a hot flash is over, it might take your mate 30 minutes or so to feel okay again. Like everything else, it depends on the woman.

Physical symptoms aside, "power surges" can also be embarrassing. For example, suddenly breaking out in a profuse sweat in front of co-workers, clients or at a social event could be a wee awkward and distracting, wouldn't you say?

The good news is that hot flashes usually stop after menopause, but 20% to 50% of women still have them for two to three years or more after their periods stop. Fortunately, their intensity decreases with time.

## A BAD NIGHT'S SLEEP

**You know a woman is in perimenopause when the phenobarbital dose that wiped out the Heaven's Gate Cult gives her four hours of decent rest.**

A lot of women have problems falling asleep, staying asleep or having a restful sleep during climate change. You're in bed with her, you know how it is. It can happen every night, or a few times a week. The extent of her insomnia can have a greater of lesser impact on her quality of life.

There are different reasons for her sleep issues, but let's start with night sweats. Your partner wakes up in a pool of sweat, hot and bothered, but not in the way you'd like. So she gets up, goes to the bathroom, gets a drink of water or a cold washcloth, or even has to change her pajamas or the sheets. Now she's awake. If she does fall back to sleep again, her night sweats can wake her three, four, five times. By morning, she's tired and cranky. Who can blame her?

**NOTE**» *MEN CAN ALSO HAVE HOT FLASHES AND NIGHT SWEATS DURING ANDROPAUSE.*

Even if your mate doesn't have night sweats, she can still have problems sleeping. Her lower estrogen levels affect her hypothalamus, which regulates her sleep cycles as well as her body heat. Her diminishing progesterone, which helps with sleep, is another cause.

## CHAIN REACTIONS

Being sleep deprived does not make women feel and operate at their best. How do you act when you're tired? Exactly. Exhausted people get irritable, moody, and have a hard time concentrating and handling everyday stresses.

So it makes sense that chronic sleeplessness can contribute to mood swings and make your lover anxious and depressed. The Catch-22 here is that those same emotions cause problems sleeping: researchers confirmed that anxiety is connected to difficulty falling asleep, and depression is connected to non-restorative sleep in peri and postmeno-pausal women. Round and round we go.

**NOTE**» *THE FDA RECOMMENDS HORMONE REPLACEMENT THERAPY TO REDUCE HOT FLASHES, NIGHT SWEATS, VAGINAL DRYNESS AND BONE LOSS IN OSTEOPOROSIS.*

Actually, replacing the diminishing estrogen and progesterone can handle almost all symptoms, but not all women need it or are willing to take it. It's a big subject, and our *Weather Protection for Women* in appendix 2 is devoted to it. Right now, just keep it in mind as an option. We recommend reading and discussing it with your partner.

## CRASHING FATIGUE

A lot of perimenopausal women complain that they're completely exhausted. And it's not just because they can't sleep. They're stressed out from their many symptoms and the resulting lack of physical and emotional energy to deal with their lives. Which brings us to cortisol.

Cortisol is produced by our adrenal glands. It converts a type of sugar that's stored in our liver and muscles (glycogen) into the form of sugar that fuels our cells (glucose) in order to sustain our energy or give us a quick energy burst when we need it. It's known as the "stress hormone" because it rushes to our rescue, increasing our energy and steadying our emotions when we're under pressure. The more stress, the more cortisol our adrenals need to make.

Climate change can raise stress levels considerably. The problem is that your mate's ebbing and imbalanced sex hormones mess up her body's ability to use cortisol efficiently, so she needs even more. Her adrenals go into overdrive trying to meet the demand, but there's a limit to how much they can make. When the demand gets to be too great and they can't produce any more, they become fatigued and exhausted. And so does your lady.

---

**CAUTION**» *CORTISOL ALSO INHIBITS IMMUNE FUNCTION.*

---

## AN ORIENTATION POINT

You may wonder why we're giving you all these biological explanations of your partner's symptoms. One reason is: why not? This is a manual, so you get to know how things work. Another is that it can be reassuring to understand that there are actual causes to this event that she's going through. She's not making it up and you're not alone in going through it with her.

Practically speaking, knowing what causes the problem can help to fix it. For example, take stress and exhausted adrenals. Obviously your partner needs to reduce the things that cause stress, but she also needs R&R. You can help by giving her a hand with the house, kids and chores. You can also encourage her to exercise. A lot of women find yoga and Pilates particularly calming and helpful.

## INSTABILITY IN THE ATMOSPHERE

*If you're looking for stability in your life, befriend a perimenopausal woman. Suddenly everything else in your life will seem rock stable.*

More than 50% of females have mood swings due to high or low estrogen and to the ensuing hormonal imbalances. This gives you a 50/50 chance of facing some pretty volatile weather. Your lover can suddenly become sad, irritable, anxious, impatient, stressed out, angry, depressed or experience an emotion that she can't even identify—like "feeling crazy". You might feel like you have to tiptoe around her, because she can get super-sensitive and overreact to something you've said or something that's happened.

---

**NOTE**» *WOMEN WHO HAD MOOD SWINGS DURING PMS OR POSTPARTUM ARE MORE LIKELY TO HAVE MOOD SWINGS DURING PERIMENOPAUSE.*

---

## CRAZY WEATHER

It's hard for a man to walk in a woman's shoes—unless he's a cross dresser. The thing to remember is that as weird and challenging as your lover's emotions can be, they are common during climate change. Because the male-dominated psychiatric profession of the 1950s never understood women in general and their change of life in particular, they used electroshock to "treat" perimenopausal emotional problems. Some still recommend it for severe depression. Aside from not addressing hormonal imbalance, which is the cause, electro-shock has two devastating potential long-term side effects: memory loss and confusion.

The problem is that there are a lot of people—many 21st century health professionals included—who still don't understand the depression, anxiety or anger that perimenopausal women might experience. It's not the sudden onset of mental illness, it's the product of a natural but potentially rough physical transition to a body that is no longer set up to make babies.

---

**WARNING**» *SOME PSYCHIATRISTS PRESCRIBE ANTI-DEPRESSANTS AND ANTI-ANXIETY DRUGS WITHOUT ENSURING THAT THEIR PATIENTS ARE RECEIVING THE RIGHT TREATMENT FOR LOW OR IMBALANCED HORMONES.*

---

Sexual side effects are common with many antidepressants. Although not all patients suffer from them, women may experience less or no desire; have fewer, no, or less intense orgasms; enjoy no or less pleasure from their orgasms; feel less clitoral or vaginal sensitivity; and have no or a diminished response to sexual stimuli. This list is depressing in itself. Therefore, it's important that antidepressants are only prescribed for the right reasons and when they're absolutely necessary.

On the encouraging side, there are now more women doctors, as well as an increase in interest and research into every stage of menopause. With understanding of menopausal symptoms on the rise, more health practitioners are referring patients to hormone specialists. If your partner is struggling but her doctor isn't helping her, encourage her to get a referral.

## DEPRESSED FRONTS

Depression was one of the conditions that inspired psychiatrists to use electroshock therapy. Today we know why perimenopausal women get the blues. It has to do with the fact that brains need estrogen to produce serotonin. Having more serotonin means being happier and more positive and feeling more pleasure. Thus, when your mate's E rises, so does her mood; when it falls, her mood follows. Low levels, particularly in women, lead to depression, sadness and anxiety.

---

**NOTE**» *DEPRESSION AND CHRONIC ANXIETY ARE MORE COMMON IN WOMEN THAN IN MEN.*

---

How come? Firstly, men have higher levels of serotonin than women. Also, while their estrogen and progesterone are in flux, ours is not. During andropause, our testosterone slowly declines and our estrogen gradually increases, which creates a whole other set of problems for guys. Depression from lack of E is not one of them.

Moreover, researchers now think that while both sexes have the same system for processing serotonin, they may use it differently. One study found that when they reduced serotonin in men's brains, they became impulsive and irritable, not depressed. Women had the opposite reaction: they not only became depressed but were more cautious.

## ON HIGH ALERT

**"I'm not tense, just terribly, terribly alert."**

It's a good thing females are wired to be cautious because they have to be vigilant to ensure their kids' survival. It's not a good thing, however, when their healthy watchfulness turns into a heightened sense of danger, leading to a persistent low-grade anxiety or apprehension, continual worry, extreme fear or panic attacks.

---

**NOTE**» WOMEN SUFFER FROM ANXIETY DISORDERS TWICE AS MUCH AS MEN DO.

---

Why does their fear escalate so much? Hormonal imbalances are a very common cause of anxiety in women in all of their weather conditions—when they're PMS, postpartum and especially in climate change. Add to that the everyday pressures of modern life: juggling a career, finances, relationship issues, taking care of kids and perhaps aging parents, and having no personal time to decompress. A lot of women get so conditioned to living in stress and anxiety that they think it's normal. Then climate change tips the scales. Adrenalin and cortisol levels rise, soothing serotonin and progesterone fall, and any anxiety they've been living with gets magnified.

Even if your mate isn't the worrying kind, all her hormonal changes can now make her vulnerable to fear. How intense it gets depends on the woman. Some women might just get a little nervous, while others can have a full blown, heart-pounding panic attack accompanied by shortness of breath, chest pains or pressure and palpitations. Now THAT is scary. Anxiety does double duty by making it hard to fall asleep and by triggering hot flashes, which of course, lead to more anxiety.

---

***NOTE»*** *MILDLY ANXIOUS WOMEN HAVE 3-5 TIMES MORE HOT FLASHES THAN THEIR NON-APPREHENSIVE SISTERS.*

---

## DECISIONS

When fear takes over our brains and bodies, it's hard to make decisions because we're terrified of the conse-quences of making the wrong ones. It feels like survival itself is at stake, even for small choices. Why? Because fear is our primal warning system, alerting us to threats to our existence. It triggers our body, making our adrenaline rocket and our hearts race. But our brains didn't evolve to recognize and turn off at imaginary dangers or override the effects of lowered or imbalanced sex hormones. We react the same way, whether the threat is real, made-up or hormonal.

That's why you need to be patient with your partner. While she knows on a rational level that which cell phone she chooses isn't life or death, it *feels* like it. If she gets nervous and can't make up her mind, lend a hand by calming her down, helping her choose, or taking some decisions off her plate.

## LOST IN THE STORM

It can be frightening to get lost if you're in unfamiliar or dangerous territory. That's when a compass, GPS, or instrument panel becomes your new best friend. But what if you don't have any way to orient yourself? That's how your lover might feel—lost, disoriented, agitated, and frightened because her inner compass isn't working. She can't find or connect to her Self anymore. And if you don't have your Self, what do you have?

This is one symptom some clients have complained about that we haven't found mentioned in the usual list of symptoms. It can be pretty traumatic. Despairing women ask questions like: "Who am I?" or fearfully state: "I don't know who I am anymore." One client described it as "an alien invasion."

A piece of advice: if she can't connect to herself, don't expect her to be good at connecting to you.

## THUNDER AND LIGHTENING

**"I'm out of estrogen and I have a gun".**

Anger rounds out the Big Three of perimenopausal weather. To clarify—there's anger and then there's *ANGER*. It's one thing when low or imbalanced hormones trigger irritability

231

and aggression. Moods swings aren't fun, but they pass. It's an entirely different dilemma, however, when the anger is deep-rooted in real-life dissatisfaction. Climate change can act like a wake-up call, alerting the woman to the fact that she's not happy with the way things are and it pisses her off. What could be wrong? A lot—particularly in terms of her relationships.

Your mate can become keenly aware of inequities: What is she getting for what she is giving? How is she being treated by you, the kids, family members, friends, or by her boss or her clients? Has she sacrificed her own needs to serve the needs of others? Is she being acknowledged for her efforts? She can feel sick and tired of putting others first and herself last.

If your partner is mad because of the dynamics of your relationship, pay attention. With everything else going on, you might be tempted to dismiss her ire as "hormonal," or worse, call her crazy. Yes, we've heard that from a few men. Aside from throwing oil on the fire, it's not true. What is happening is that her body is transitioning and so is she. It's like a mid-life crisis in that she's driven to reinvent herself–and with that, your relationship.

It's a good time for couple's counseling or coaching. Guys can resent going to a counselor because they feel they're being forced to do it. But unwillingness to talk about issues or dealing with their mate's needs could be what's provoking her in the first place. And once they're involved in the process, men usually find that they've got some grievances of their own. If having a happy relationship is the goal, both partners need to confront and deal with unhealthy patterns and unresolved issues. If they don't, "for better or worse" may no longer be an option.

---

***WARNING***» *ONE IN FOUR DIVORCES IS BETWEEN COUPLES 50 AND OLDER—MOST OF THEM INITIATED BY WOMEN.*

---

Hopefully, forewarned is forearmed on the emotional front. Most likely nothing drastic will occur, and with your new "emotional intelligence" you'll be able to weather whatever comes your way.

Next up: your lover's cognitive challenges.

---

***NOTE***» *AS MANY AS 60% OF PERIMENOPAUSAL WOMEN HAVE MEMORY AND COGNITIVE PROBLEMS.*

---

## MEMORY CHIPS

***You know your wife is in climate change when she writes Post-it notes with your kids' names on them.***

Have you noticed your mate forgetting things more often, like:

- Why she came into the room?
- What she just did?
- Words?

- Appointments?

- Locations?

- Faces of acquaintances?

- How to do routine tasks, such as how to use her cell phone camera or the windshield wipers on her car?

Are you afraid she might be on her way to early Alzheimer's but don't want to mention it for the obvious reasons? Well, if it makes you feel better, she's probably secretly freaking out about the same thing.

Fortunately, you're both wrong; the intermittent memory loss is the result of the huge impact that estrogen withdrawal is having on her brain. Why? Because E is integral to learning and to forming and preserving long- and short-term memories. It affects everything from how her brain cells are structured to how they connect, the electrical and chemical interactions between them, and the strength of memory grooves.

---

*CAUTION*» *SOME DOCTORS DO MISDIAGNOSE THE COGNITIVE SYMPTOMS AS EARLY ALZHEIMER'S OR ADULT ATTENTION DEFICIT DISORDER.*

---

## BLINKING AWARENESS

You need to be present to learn or to remember anything. That means you have to be able to pay attention and to focus. But your lover can have trouble concentrating, get distracted, or sporadically blank out for a few seconds or more. If she's looking but not seeing, she's not recording and has no memory in the first place.

## BRAIN FOG

It isn't just her failing memory that can give your lover dark Alzheimer fantasies. It's also trying to navigate through the thick, cottony, heavy fog that fills her brain. Words and information disappear in the mist; connecting thoughts into coherent sentences becomes difficult, so she has to struggle to express herself verbally—something women are definitely not used to.

## POOR VISIBILITY

While it might be safe having these lapses at home, being inarticulate and forgetting things don't go over so well at work or with clients. Add to these the potential for:

- Losing her train of thought

- Thoughts getting blocked

- Problems prioritizing

- Not grasping what she's reading

Now your smart woman feels stupid. It's very demoralizing and stressful, especially if her job depends on her clarity and mental acuity.

---

**NOTE**» *ALTHOUGH WOMEN FROM DIFFERENT
RACES SEEM TO SUFFER FROM DIFFERENT
PHYSICAL SYMPTOMS MORE THAN OTHERS,
THEY ALL EXPERIENCE COGNITIVE PROBLEMS.*

---

Why does the disruption of estrogen make so many women from so many cultures feel like they're losing their minds?

## *BRAIN FUEL*

Just like you can't fly a jet without fuel, your brain can't function without its fuels: glucose and oxygen. Your brain has a big appetite. Although it is just 2% of your weight, your blood vessels transport 20% of your body's blood supply to it. And for good reason: without glucose your brain cells can't work, and without oxygen your brain cells die.

---

**NOTE**» *ESTROGEN INCREASES BLOOD FLOW
AND THE ACCESSIBILITY OF GLUCOSE AND
OXYGEN TO OUR BRAINS.*

---

Less estrogen means less blood flow, glucose, and oxygen, so your partner's brain has less energy to do its job. Because her E can fluctuate as her climate changes, your mate can have intermittent cognitive troubles. It's worse if her E bottoms out and the problems are steady.

The other thing to know is that estrogen boosts the brain chemicals that keep the cells talking to each other.

Less E = less communication = less coordination = more problems thinking.

## SUDDEN WEIGHT GAIN

**"I'm out of estrogen – but I have chocolate!"**

Another thing that can mess with your lover's mind is sudden weight gain. Adding 10-20 pounds and a fatter, rounder tummy is one of the most common woes of decreasing estrogen and progesterone.

## WHY IS SHE GAINING WEIGHT?

You know how it is when you're home and you crave something sweet or salty and you think you're out of it? You search through cabinets or anywhere you think you may have something stashed. Well, that's what your lover's body does. When her ovaries are shutting down, and it's hungry for E, her body finds it in secondary sources: her adrenal glands, skin, and in this case, her fat cells.

If fat cells are a reliable new source, the body reasons it makes sense to make more of them. So your mate can feel hungrier and consume more. Even a good diet and exercise might not be enough for her to keep her figure, though. Her body may produce more fat cells anyway. It so unfair!

And let's not forget bloating, since declining proges-terone can make your mate retain water. What's a lovely lady to do? It's stressful to watch your waist and tummy expand—which, of course, only makes matters worse.

---

**NOTE**» *CORTISOL, THE STRESS HORMONE,
BLOCKS WEIGHT LOSS.*

---

What's a guy to do? Your lover's self-esteem could be decreasing with each unwanted pound. One consequence can be that she feels too unattractive to have sex, which is something you definitely don't want to happen. Love her, comfort her, and encourage her to eat healthy food and exercise no matter what. Healthy women are beautiful.

## PARCHED SKIN

Dry skin is another morale buster. An abundance of E receptors in your partner's skin makes it moist and radiant during her fertile years. Throughout climate change her E-thirsty skin loses moisture, producing more wrinkles on her pretty face. She can also have less lubrication in her vagina which, as you will see, makes sex painful.

Which brings us to the burning question: will your sex life suffer during perimenopause?

## SEX

On the sunny side, maybe you'll get lucky. Your lover could be one of those women whose climate change is barely noticeable or mild, so your sex and relationship life aren't affected at all. Or, oh happy day, she could be one of the few women whose libido actually increases. Many couples, however, are not so fortunate.

---

**NOTE**» *ABOUT 50% OF WOMEN HAVE A DECREASE OR LOSS OF SEX DRIVE DURING PERIMENOPAUSE.*

---

## WHY DOESN'T YOUR LOVER WANT SEX?

You may have been here before when your mate's hormones were unbalanced—during PMS, pregnancy or postpartum. If your woman is grappling with a bunch of stressful symptoms that exhaust, depress or mess with her mind, she's just not going to be in the mood. And feeling fat and unattractive are not exactly aphrodisiacs.

But there could be other causes as well. A woman's libido is a complex mix of hormones, health, feeling good about herself, having an emotional connection with her partner, and having time and energy.

You need to take a look and see if the stressors we talked about in the anxiety section, health issues, or medicines are damaging her sex drive. You also need to get real about any relationship problems that existed before perimenopause. Did you both put in the time and energy to communicate and to create love and intimacy? Have you drifted from lovers to just friends? Are you sort of living separate lives together? Is there hostility? We've seen couples where it was hormones plus some or all of the above. If you want a good sex life, you have to face and correct whatever problems exist.

That being said, you could also be having a good sex and relationship life when, out of the blue, her libido nose dives. Do not panic! Do not blame her! Here's what's happening.

## REASONS

Your lover's ovaries produce all her sex hormones—progesterone, estrogen and testosterone—and they all play a big part in her sexual response. Since they are declining in their own imbalanced way, it's logical to expect that she might have some sexual problems.

And remember that it was the rising of estrogen and testosterone in the middle of your lover's cycle that made her predictably hot, horny and ready to conceive. Although neither of you will bemoan the loss of her periods, you sure might miss that monthly spike in her libido.

---

**NOTE**» *LOSS OF DESIRE DOESN'T NECESSARILY MEAN YOUR PARTNER CAN'T ENJOY SEX.*

---

Without Nature getting her hot, it's more important than ever for both of you to create the connection and the environment to turn her on. That and great foreplay might be all she needs to get aroused and to experience deep and satisfying sex, but it may not be all.

## WHAT'S TESTOSTERONE GOT TO DO WITH IT?

While estrogen and progesterone are part and parcel of your lover's sexual response, the Big T drives it. She needs enough of "the hormone of desire" to have healthy sexual activity, which includes sexual craving, arousal, pleasure and orgasm.

---

**NOTE**» *SOME WOMEN HAVE PROBLEMS ACHIEVING ORGASM DURING PERIMENOPAUSE.*

---

When it comes to pleasure, it's your lover's testosterone that makes her nipples and clitoris sensitive. And, as you're undoubtedly aware, a sensitive clitoris is key to orgasm.

## DECLINING TESTOSTERONE

T declines in women as well as in men. By the time she's in perimenopause, your lover is producing at least half of what she did when she was 20. The decline is even more severe if your mate has had a hysterectomy because most of her testosterone is produced in her ovaries. If she's stressed out, her T levels also suffer. And there's nothing like hot flashes, sleepless night, mood swings and dysfunctional brains to raise a woman's stress levels.

## CAN YOU DO ANYTHING ABOUT IT?

There's been a lot of research about what happens when you add testosterone to estrogen and progesterone in hormone replacement therapy. The results generally show big improvements in every aspect of sexual response. Read more about it in Appendix 2, *Weather Protection For Women.*

## LUBE IT OR LOSE IT

Estrogen brings blood to your mate's vagina, making it wet, juicy, and pleasurable. When estrogen declines, her lovely pussy can become dry, and her vaginal walls can thin due to her tissue shrinking, causing itching, soreness, discomfort or pain. It can feel like sandpaper to her and sting when you enter. Who wants sex under those conditions? Not her, not you.

If your woman's discomfort is mild, she can try using vitamin E suppositories twice a week and eating more estrogen-rich soy products. Generally, water-soluble lubes, like Sylk, Astroglide, K-Y jelly or all natural alternatives decrease the friction, but there could still be pain because they don't address the thinning walls. Hormone replacement is the gold standard for relieving menopausal sexual troubles, especially vaginal dryness. But if your lover is afraid of it, she can try *Vagifem*, a pill with a small dose of estrogen that's inserted into the vagina and acts locally, so there's very little E that goes into the bloodstream. Or, she can try a small dose of

242

an estrogen cream or testosterone. Even for women with a history of breast cancer, using a small amount of cream will not increase the risk. She also needs to be drinking lots of water to keep her mucous membrane moist.

## RESPONSIVENESS

Regarding sexual sensitivity, being wet isn't necessarily a sign that your woman is turned on. Do you know what is? The swelling of her inner and outer vaginal area, including her lips, clitoris and G-spot. Her whole vaginal area is composed of erectile tissue and when it is engorged with blood, it is oh so sensitive, incredibly pleasurable and builds to orgasm. That's just like what happens to your penis when you have a hard-on. Thus, if her E decreases and less blood flows to her vagina, there can be a lessening in her erectile response, her sensitivity and pleasure.

There's no problem if your lover will do hormone replacement, but again, if she doesn't want to, she could at least ask her doctor about using estrogen in the form of vaginal rings and creams. They boost that all-important blood flow, helping to heighten her sensitivity, which in turn makes it easier for her to climax.

## USE IT OR LOSE IT

Exercise builds muscles and increases blood flow. This holds true for your lover's intimate parts. Stimulating her vagina and intercourse increase her blood flow, exercise her vaginal muscles, and create healthier tissue, wall linings and more lubrication. Counter-intuitively, it's particularly important to exercise her vaginal muscles if just using a lube doesn't handle the pain.

---

**NOTE**» *HAVING SEX LESS FREQUENTLY CAN RESULT IN HAVING MORE PAIN DURING INTERCOURSE.*

---

What can she do? Religiously practice her *kegels*, which is contracting and releasing her vaginal muscles. She may have done this during or after pregnancy to prevent leaking urine.

What can you do? Back to foreplay, always a requisite for turning your lover on and swelling her erectile tissue. After caressing, kissing her all over, gently stroking her pussy, and/ or delicately performing oral sex, add lube and estrogen cream and there's a good chance she'll be ready for intercourse.

## *WHAT IF IT IS STILL TOO PAINFUL FOR INTERCOURSE?*

Luckily there's mutual oral sex and masturbation for pleasure, satisfaction and connection. If at all possible, don't go without.

## MORE CHALLENGES

As if there aren't enough challenges to having sex with your lover during climate change, here are two more: low E can make your women more susceptible to urinary or vaginal infections.

Throw in the loss of tissue tone, and your mate may also have leaking urine or loss of bladder control, as well the need to urinate more—all the more reason for kegels and sex.

## WEATHER GEAR

If there ever was a time a woman needs a trusted doctor, conventional or alternative, this is it. By "trusted" we mean someone who is an expert on perimenopause and postmenopause and gets results. It seems like a no-brainer but women often don't know who to go to, or they stay with a doctor who isn't really helping them. Your partner could need a little push to find the right one. Sometimes women like to use a combination of conventional and alterative remedies. Whatever it takes, having the appropriate care can turn stormy weather into sunny days.

If your mate goes to a conventional doctor, she might get a prescription for Hormone Replacement Therapy (HRT) or Bioidentical Hormone Replacement Therapy (BHRT). As we've pointed out, hormone replacement is the most effective proven treatment for menopausal symptoms available, but your partner may not need it or want it. If she does need it, but is afraid of side effects, it's a good idea for both of you to read *Weather Protection For Women*. In it, we discuss her choices for treatment, the pros and cons of each, current research, and the safest ways to use HRT or BHRT. As many of us have learned, we need to take responsibility for our own knowledge and healing. So even if she has a doctor and is already on HRT or BHRT, the chapter has important information she may not be aware of but should know.

Alternative doctors may or may not be able to prescribe HRT or BHRT. They might also have herbal options that work on women who have milder symptoms or just need a tweak. On the Oriental medicine front, there's acupuncture as well as herbs.

If your lover's only problem is hot flashes, she can see if red clover, flaxseed, black cohosh or dong quai work for her. Exercise, a panacea to all our ills, also reduces hot flashes as well as insomnia, mood swings, and fatigue. Additionally, it boosts sex drive, erotic pleasure, self-image and just feeling good. Definitely get her to exercise.

## *MENOPAUSE*

It is one year to the day after your mate's last period. Hello postmenopause and the rest of her life.

Her body hasn't stopped making E. It's making dramatically less, getting it from other sources, like her adrenals, skin and body fat, and using a different kind.

---

**NOTE**» *FROM NOW ON, WHEN WE TALK ABOUT E, WE'RE TALKING ABOUT ESTRONE, WHICH IS WEAKER THAN THE ESTRADIOL SHE PRODUCED WHEN SHE WAS FERTILE.*

---

## CLIMATE CHANGED

The average age of menopause for American women is around 52 and they generally live to their early 80s. Think about it: that's 28+ years to enjoy their retirement from fertility and monthly cycles. What does that mean, physically and psychologically, to them and to their relationships? As you might expect, it means different things to different women.

## CLIMATE ASSESSMENT

Your partner now has dramatically less sex hormones, and her body may or may not be able to adjust to the new status quo so that she feels good. Any of the perimenopausal symptoms she had due to lowered or imbalanced estrogen, progesterone and testosterone can continue. Or new ones, which we associate with "aging" can crop up. That is, unless she is using HRT or BHRT to control them. If your lover replaced her hormones during perimenopause and still does, her symptoms should continue to be under control. If she starts shortly after climate change, she'll also find relief from many of her symptoms.

This leaves the vast majority of women who didn't replace their hormones and never will, and those who used them and stopped. What about them?

As in perimenopause, some women may have no symptoms, only one, or their own personal assortment of symptoms in varying intensities. The main difference now is that some of their symptoms may lessen or go away completely as the years go by, while others may linger or get worse.

Given your lover's personal climate, you need to watch how her body is handling her symptoms over time. Here's some general information that might help.

## MILD WEATHER

Let's say your partner didn't have any symptoms during perimenopause or she had mild ones that she could tolerate or handle with exercise, herbs or alternative therapy. Her postmenopause can be a breeze. Her weather will probably stay fairly mild, although sometimes troubling new symptoms can surprise her. More on those shortly.

## HOT AND HUMID

Your partner might be one of the 30%-80% of women who get hot flashes and night sweats.

---

**NOTE**» *30%-80% IS A BIG RANGE. THERE'S NO ONE PERCENTAGE BECAUSE DIFFERENT TRIALS AND TESTS COME UP WITH DIFFERENT NUMBERS.*

---

They also vary in strength and in the number of years they last. If hot flashes and night sweats were your mate's major complaint, she could in fact, be overjoyed that there was a dramatic drop in their intensity once her periods stopped. It's amazing how much better life looks when she's not waking up dripping wet multiple times a night. She might even feel what Margaret Mead termed "menopausal zest"—a renewed energy and enthusiasm for life.

While many women can expect the heat to end after two to three years, others can experience it for seven to ten years. This may not be as bad as it sounds because her hot flashes and night sweats may not be as strong to begin with and they decrease in number and frequency before eventually stopping.

But it can be pretty harsh for some women. In one test, researchers found 29% of women had severe hot flashes that hit their highest point after their periods stopped and lasted 10+ years.

On to sleep.

# RESTLESS NIGHTS

Your woman could still be stumbling around exhausted during the day because she can't fall or stay asleep or have a restful night's sleep. Or this could be a brand new problem because more women have sleep disturbances after climate change than before it.

---

**NOTE»** UP TO 60% OF POSTMENOPAUSAL WOMEN HAVE SLEEP DISTURBANCES.

---

Night sweats, feeling depressed or anxious, illness, medications, including the psychiatric drugs she's taking to deal with her emotions, can keep her tossing and turning. Another reason could be closer to home: impotence is a source of female depression and sleep problems. Losing your lover is heartbreaking.

# HANDLING THE CHALLENGING WEATHER

Here we have a common menopause/andropause relationship challenge. The *erectile dysfunction (ED)* could be caused by Low T, a hormonal imbalance, medications, psychological, or relationship issues. While a man can be powerless to help with his lover's hot flashes and night sweats, he can do something about his own impotence. It's a simple Two Step process:

1. *Research doctors or therapists who specialize in and successfully treat ED issues.*
2. *Go.*

Some men refuse to talk about it or handle the problem. This does not make the issue go away. What it can do is make their hopeless mates lose respect and go away—permanently.

If you are suffering from ED, please remember that it is communication and mutual support that make a winning team and that solving this problem can bring you together. Aside from therapeutic or medical solutions, intimacy is in itself a turn on. You can still engage in foreplay, connect, and satisfy her by giving her oral sex or using a dildo or her vibrator. Whether you ejaculate or not, you can kiss, feel sensations in your body, watch her orgasm and enjoy the closeness. You'll both be happier and sleep better.

## IS YOUR SEX LIFE GOOD BUT SHE'S STILL AWAKE?

Another cause for your partner's sleep issues is that *melatonin*, the brain chemical that tells the body it's time to sleep, declines with age. However, if your partner uses hormone replacement, she'll have a distinct advantage. A trial of 3,128 postmenopausal women found that hormone users had the best sleep, followed by women who had used them but stopped. Women who never used hormone replacement slept the worse.

## FATIGUED?

Is it age or hormones? Probably both, but up to 88% of women say they experience it. Maybe you do too.

## MOODY WEATHER

**You know a woman is in postmenopause when everyone around her has an attitude.**

Yes, mood swings can continue or start once your partner's climate has changed. About 20% to 66% of women have them. That's another big range, but it does indicate a definite problem. Thus, the "grumpy old man" from andropause might find himself mated with a "very irritated old woman."

## DEPRESSED FRONTS

Was your mate depressed or anxious during climate change? The forecast is that she'll continue to be down or apprehensive if she wasn't treated earlier. Why? Because her low E and progesterone still cause low production of the brain chemicals she needs to feel calm and happy.

Here's another heartfelt plea: if your partner is still feeling hopeless, persistently sad or frightened, we entreat you to help her get the treatment she needs.

## STILL FOGGY

Alas, your partner's haze may not lift after menopause. In fact, it can get worse, at least for a while. The

National Institute of Health recently studied mental capability from the start of perimenopause through the first 12 months after menopause. They discovered that women's ability to pay attention, learn, retain and use new verbal information declines the most during that first year. So does their speed at using the fine motor skills that enable them to do valuable things like use their cell phones and computers, and most importantly, apply their makeup. Unfortunately, the test didn't continue into the second year or beyond.

So what's the forecast? While a number of researchers and many women say cognitive problems linger, others find they fade with time. One group that seems to continue to have them, however, is women with osteoporosis. A new study showed that postmenopausal women who have low bone density also have cognitive problems.

## THE WEIGHT THING

**"I'm in shape. Round is a shape, isn't it?"**

It is, and you might be seeing more of it. Look around at the women 50+ or at your lover. Or at yourself in the mirror – but that's in the andropause chapter. Back to her: if she didn't gain 10-20 pounds in perimenopause, she can now. Her body's strategy to get more E by retaining and multiplying fat cells has some pluses.

---

**NOTE**» *HEAVIER WOMEN WHO WERE 60+*
*TEND TO HAVE FEWER HOT FLASHES THAN*
*LEANER WOMEN.*

---

They also have fewer wrinkles. The downside is, of course, all the illnesses associated with being overweight, including diabetes and heart disease.

## DROUGHT

**"There is always a lot to be grateful for. Right now I'm sitting here thinking how nice it is that wrinkles don't hurt."**

So true, because desert conditions make E-thirsty skin drier, more wrinkled and less elastic. They also make your mate's hair drier, duller and thinner. A shout out to the manufacturers of anti-aging moisturizers, hair products and cosmetic treatments for their ceaseless labor to combat these ills—but they can only do so much. It can be very disheartening.

## VAGINAL DRYNESS

What can be even more disheartening to both of you is when your lover's vagina becomes dry as Death Valley, because it can mean death to your sex life. This falls into the "things get worse" after menopause category. Unfortunately, only a tiny minority of women escape this one.

## MORE PROBLEMS

Also bad news for your sex life is the increased risk postmenopausal women have for getting vaginal, urinary tract, and bladder infections. Arid conditions create a two-pronged threat: Firstly, estrogen withdrawal causes your mate's genital tissue to thin and shrink. When it thins down to a single cell, it can get microscopic tears, especially when you enter. Secondly, vaginal fluid needs E to maintain its acidity and without it bacteria thrive. Those tears enable the bacteria to get into her body and travel up to her urethra and bladder.

## WHOOPS

Since one of E's many jobs is to keep your partner's bladder muscles strong, desert weather can cause stress incontinence, which is a loss of bladder control when your mate does certain physical activities, laughs, coughs, sneezes, or climaxes. Up to 40% of postmenopausal women deal with this. Encourage her to do her kegels; not only will her strengthened pelvic floor muscles prevent leaking, but they can also give your penis a very stimulating squeeze.

Which brings us to ...

## SEX

Do you know the joke about climate change? Think globally, act locally, panic internally? Here are some scary statistics from the Mayo Clinic's Proceedings on Sexual

Dysfunction to trigger your inner freak-out. They found that 87% of married postmenopausal women in their study experienced decreased desire, 83% had difficulty climaxing, 74% had poor lubrication, and 71% felt discomfort when they made love. Shoot me now.

A scarcity of sex hormones after menopause can cause more of the libido-busting troubles we detailed in perimenopause. However, that's only part of the problem; the statistics also reflect the stress in these women's lives, their physical condition, the state of their relationships, and their mate's potency and lovemaking skills. Plus, as couples age, they have more health issues and take more medications to manage them. Both have a huge impact: you don't feel turned on when you're not feeling well and many drugs inhibit desire, arousal, ability to perform, pleasure and orgasm.

## NO LIBIDO

A "decrease in desire" can mean anything from a little to a lot. A nosedive in desire sounds the alarm. Even formerly lusty ladies might find themselves completely disinterested. Don't worry, it's probably not you; it's usually hormonal and it's very common. Here's a welcome ray of light in the midst of the gloom:

**NOTE**» *USUALLY WOMEN WHO HAD A VIBRANT, SATISFYING SEX LIFE BEFORE MENOPAUSE CONTINUE TO HAVE ONE AFTERWARD.*

Why? Because love, sex and relationships are important to these erotic females and they do whatever it takes to keep their libido alive and well. When they need help, they run to their health professionals, conventional or alternative, to get it. This is often the time when many decide to start hormone or bioidentical hormone replacement and/or testosterone replacement to restore drive, sensitivity and all their other intimate pleasures. They might also get more proactive about their health by losing weight, working out and eating better.

**WARNING**» *IF SEX WASN'T GOOD DUE TO STRESS, AN UNHAPPY RELATIONSHIP, NOT BEING SATISFIED, ETC., YOUR LOVER MIGHT NOT CARE ABOUT SEX, OR BE GLAD IT'S OVER.*

If that is the case, and you want sex with her, it's time for you to take a look at what you're doing or not doing to contribute to the problem. Couples counseling would be a valuable start.

## ARE THERE ETHNIC OR CULTURAL DIFFERENCES?

Yes. Using white women for the basis of comparison: African American women have intercourse more often; Chinese, Japanese and Hispanic women are less aroused; Hispanic women feel less pleasure; and Asian women feel more pain.

## PAINFUL SEX

"Discomfort in sex" covers a range of feeling. Pain is more explicit. Studies find that 25%-45% of postmenopausal women find sex painful, mostly due to vaginal dryness. Hopefully your lover is not among them. If she is, will she tell you? Fix it? Or stop having intercourse? Not necessarily.

A revealing online survey of 1,043 postmenopausal women by *Healthy Women* discovered that 93% of the women who said they were in pain still had intercourse, and 40% made love once a week or more. Ouch. Of those, 73% of them only did it to please their partner.

## WHY WOULDN'T SHE TELL YOU?

You'd think she would, wouldn't you? However, according to that same survey, many women were too embarrassed to talk to their lovers about their vaginal and sexual symptoms. What's more startling is they were also too self-conscious to tell their health professionals.

We've seen this in couple's counseling. One husband and wife were on the verge of divorce because he was desperate for sex and felt rejected. On the rare occasions they had it, she did it to appease him. Nevertheless, it was like pulling teeth to get her to tell him about her vaginal symptoms because she felt "too uncomfortable." She also hadn't discussed them with her gynecologist. And this was a very well educated, upper middle-class, working mom.

---

*NOTE» HE DIDN'T THINK SHE WAS IN PAIN BECAUSE SHE WAS WET, BUT AS WE'VE POINTED OUT, THAT DIDN'T MEAN SHE WAS LUBRICATED OR TURNED ON.*

---

The other reason why women just lived with their symptoms was because they didn't think they could be helped, medically or otherwise—which as you know by now is not true.

---

*NOTE» THIS IS WHY YOU AND YOUR LOVER SHOULD READ THIS CHAPTER TOGETHER AND WHY YOU HAVE TO ASK QUESTIONS.*

---

## GREAT SEX

On the sunny side, more than half of men and women 50 and older continue to have sex. In a recent US survey, that percentage held until they were 75, after which 20% remained sexually active. How often do they make love? According to another survey, 22% of those grey and silver-haired lovers had sex once a week or more; 28% made love once a month or more. Not bad considering we know a lot of younger couples that would envy those seniors.

As you've read, some of the women in the surveys might have just been accommodating their partners, but as you've also read a lot of them might be having a great time in bed. A number of ladies are also joyfully proclaiming that they're having the best sex of their lives after menopause. Who are these free-spirited goddesses? Why are they so lucky?

Beyond having a gratifying, loving partner, a good life, and taking responsibility for their sexuality, they could:

- Have good DNA

- Have strong adrenals pumping out an ample supply of sex hormones

- Have naturally high testosterone and be testosterone dominant

- Be using HRT or BHRT

- Be using estrogen-based vaginal pills, rings or creams

- Be using testosterone

- Found alternative therapies to manage the symptoms that crash their sex lives

    They're also...

## FREE AT LAST

The passionate women of postmenopause are living in a new climate that frees up their energy. No PMS, cramps and monthly bleeding, no contraceptives and worrying about pregnancy. If they had kids and they're out of the house, there's finally time and space to explore their sexuality.

## IN PRAISE OF OLDER WOMEN

Experience and confidence pay off in bed. Unlike the ladies who felt it was taboo to discuss their needs, these sensualists of "a certain age" ask for what they want. So be prepared to up the ante. They might also have reached the point where they're more experimental and adventurous. *A blessing: may your lover be one of them.*

If your mate's libido is alive and well, you could have the added pleasure of seeing her have more orgasms and multi-orgasms than she had before menopause.

## ENJOYING HER NEW CLIMATE

Whether you call it a "rite of passage" or "2nd midlife crisis", the fact is that your partner may have a new perspective on who she is now and how she wants to live her life. It's a powerful place for the modern woman to be. She has a lot more options than earlier generations of women because of her hard-earned experience, psychology and expectations. Your partner and many of her postmenopausal sisters were trailblazers who pushed the boundaries for all females. They made love not war, explored their sexuality, got educated, worked in fields previously closed to women, found satisfaction and respect in their careers, handled their own finances, and raised families. They're independent, confident and believe they're entitled to be happy and fulfilled. And many of them will do their damnedest to achieve those goals. Sort of like you.

This is not to say your partner doesn't have her insecurities and conflicts. Who doesn't? But this woman is entering another phase of her life. It's very likely she is reevaluating her past and redefining both her purposes and her relationship roles. Her postmenopausal reality plays a big part in who she is becoming.

## UPGRADED MODEL

Your lover's desire to put less focus on pleasing, caring and nurturing others that began in perimenopause solidifies in postmenopause. Now she has few qualms about pleasing, caring and nurturing herself.

In case you're wondering what's going on in that pretty brain of hers, this is it. Your mate's brain's structures and circuits that made her so sensitive to other people's emotions and needs are still there, but they're only being fueled by a fraction of the E they used to get. Ditto for the circuits for sweet oxytocin that pushed her to bond and were ignited and amplified by E. As far as Mother Nature is concerned, no more babies, and no more need to gas up the parts of your partner's brain that kept her on track as a mother.

---

**NOTE**» *TO KEEP HER ON TRACK AS A LOVER, GAZING IN HER EYES, TALKING, STROKING, HUGS, KISSING AND ORGASMS STILL REV UP THE OXYTOCIN.*

---

## EXPLORING HER INNER-MALE

It's been commonly noted that men mellow and women toughen as they age. The hormonal truth behind those observations is that men become estrogen-dominant in andropause and women can become testosterone-dominant in postmenopause. How does the latter affect your mate?

Have you noticed that she has a shorter fuse? Another brain change is that your partner's anger channels are becoming more like a guy's. Be nice. Payback can be a bitch.

You might also have noticed that she has become more aggressive, adventurous, independent, risk taking, goal-oriented and focused on getting what she wants—all characteristics of testosterone. Although your lover has less testosterone than ever, the proportion of her T to her E can be as much as 20 times higher than it was in her fertile years. Of course she doesn't become a man, but she can begin thinking and acting more like one.

Don't be surprised if she stops cooking, insists on nights out, goes back to school, starts her own business, changes careers, or takes up skydiving. The point is, it's a time for changes and she's got the energy and drive to make them. Try to stop her at your peril.

## GREY DIVORCE

**Susan: Aren't you wearing your wedding ring on the wrong finger?**

**Barbara: Yes. I married the wrong man.**

If she's postmenopausal, Barbara may not stay married to him for long. We already warned you that a quarter of divorces are from couples over 50, and 65% of them are initiated by women. That's not even counting splits by the couples in committed relationships or those who are dating.

What this tells you is that many postmenopausal women are deadly serious about being emotionally supported and not settling for unhappy relationships. Their hormones are influencing them to be more assertive, less willing to suppress their needs in order to keep the family together, and less willing to avoid conflicts. It's a frame of mind that's here to stay.

Is your relationship in danger? Not if it was healthy to begin with. If you love, support, and trust each other and have good communication and problem-solving skills, your partner's new attitudes are no big deal. She explores her masculine side, you explore your new feminine side; she does new things and you do new things, independently or together. You both adapt. No worries.

## *WORRIES*

If your relationship is troubled and your partner is unhappy, watch out for severe weather. Here are some potential doomsday scenarios:

- You've been cheating and she knows it

- You're relationship has been hostile or dead for years

- You or she is just waiting for the kids to go to college so you can break up

If these describe you, you might want to make a list of your assets and start researching a good divorce lawyer.

If you're not there yet, but any of the following ring a bell, a storm might be brewing that could leave you single in its wake.

- You're ignoring what she's feeling or wants to do

- You're putting down her ideas/needs/plans/ ambitions, as usual

- She says she wants to change; you insist things stay the same

- She's threatened divorce before but never followed through, so you think she's bluffing

- She says she wants a divorce for the first time and you think she's bluffing

- You won't communicate about the issues or go to therapy to deal with them

Provided that you don't underestimate your mate, you might still have time to save your relationship. Make it your mission. Show up, stop resisting, start listening, and support her. It could take a lot of work to break old habits, like having to be right all the time and avoiding responsibility for your part of the problem. So what? You should deal with your flaws anyway and learn to be a better partner. Plus, it will take a lot more effort to deal with an emotionally and financially difficult divorce.

It's worth it. There are plenty of really happy older couples that finally worked through their problems and went on to enjoy each other like never before. You could be one of them.

## HEALTH FORECAST

Older couples generally live longer than singles because, amongst other things, they become each other's health coach and take care of each other. In that light, here's a heads up on the two most prevalent illnesses associated with depleted estrogen: osteoporosis and heart disease. These subjects are too big to cover in this chapter, but we thought we should at least give you some information. If your partner is at risk or is afflicted with either, naturally you'll want to research it in depth.

Another reason why we're alerting you to these illnesses is because HRT or BHRT can be employed to treat them. The FDA approves their use for osteoporosis—which is why many postmenopausal women choose to stay on hormone therapy. There's an ongoing debate amongst health practitioners and researchers about their risks and benefits. It's all in Appendix 2, *Weather Protection For Women.*

## *OSTEOPOROSIS*

If your mate tells you she has osteoporosis, pay attention. Defined as porous bones, it is the result of bone tissue breaking down much faster than it is rebuilding. sSince E is a key factor in building women's bones, bone loss and softening can occur after menopause. After the age of 65, 25% of women are afflicted with osteoporosis and it gets progressively worse over the years.

---

**NOTE**» *MEN CAN ALSO GET OSTEOPOROSIS, BUT INITIALLY GET IT ABOUT HALF AS OFTEN AS WOMEN. AFTER THEY REACH 75, 25% OF MEN ALSO HAVE IT.*

---

Weak bones are the reason why so many women over 50 get hip fractures. As a matter of fact, your mate may have a one in seven chance of breaking her hip. That might not sound so drastic, but take a look at the statistics. After their fall:

- 24% die of complications a year later

- 50% need to use a cane or walker

- 53% of patients 65+ go directly from the hospital to a long-term care facility

---

**NOTE**» *SLENDER, SMALL-BONED WHITE AND ASIAN WOMEN HAVE THE HIGHEST RISK. HISPANIC WOMEN HAVE LESS, AND AFRICAN-AMERICANS HAVE THE LEAST— 1/3 THAT OF WHITE WOMEN.*

---

Fragile bones can also lead to dangerous fractures in your mate's wrist and spine.

## HEALTH COACH

There's a lot that can be done for osteoporosis. Hormone replacement and certain medications build bones. Lifestyle changes also make a considerable difference.

Encourage your partner to: get a gym membership because weight bearing exercise builds bones; get out into the sun because sunlight creates Vitamin D, which is vital for bone health; and take calcium and Vitamin D supplements. And of course, stop smoking or drinking too much as both are huge risk factors.

# HEART DISEASE

This is the #1 killer of postmenopausal women. Although they generally get heart disease 10 years later than guys, females have the same risk for it by the time they're 65. Another scary statistic is that 400,000 American women die of heart disease each year.

Evidence points to E being heart protective. Having a strong, positive effect on your lover's cardiovascular system and blood vessels, it boosts good and reduces bad cholesterol; boosts blood flow by relaxing and enlarging blood vessels; and gets rid of free radicals, a normal but destructive by-product of cell processes. Free radicals injure cells and speed up the advancement of cardiovascular disease.

Other factors, however, greatly increase your mate's risk of having a heart attack: Is there a history of heart disease in her family? Does she eat a high fat, high salt diet? Does she drink too much? Smoke? Is she continually stressed out? Is she obese?

As her health coach, you know the drill. Neither of you can do anything about heredity, but you can support her in taking charge of unhealthy habits. You want to keep her precious heart beating.

# LOVE IN A NEW CLIMATE

We said your mate is part of a social revolution, but so are you. And together you've changed gender and relationship roles and rules. Unlike your parents, you've also reached out for sex and relationship help. Record numbers of men and women are reading books and magazines, going to therapy to deal with their baggage, attending seminars to learn how to find a mate or be better partners, and to couples counseling to fix their problems.

Now here you are again, at the forefront of a revolution in aging. Historically, there were always some genetically blessed individuals who lived long lives, but the vast majority did not. Life expectancy in the United States was 47 in 1900, 68 in 1950, and now averages 77.97 years. Many people are living well into their 80s and 90s. They're also dating, forming committed relationships, staying in long-term relationships and marriages, divorcing, and recommitting again—en masse.

What does that mean? For one thing, that relationship skills are more important than ever. And congratulations for learning about what makes your partner tick. That will definitely help.

It also means that there's a whole new model of possibility. You've got all this wisdom and experience and now you also have the gift of time. You can use what you've learned to get what you've always wanted. If you haven't been able to create a good relationship, you can do it now. If you and your partner are already happy, how much deeper can you go? How much more love can you create? How much better can it get?

It's thrilling to imagine the emotional fulfillment you can achieve and the creativity you can unleash. Successful relationships empower couples in their inner and outer worlds. What will you do? Personally and together? Who knows? It's a new frontier. First time—en masse—remember. Our vision is optimistic. We believe you can have the most fulfilling and rewarding love, sex and relationship of your life. And lead the way for others.

# THE PERI AND POSTMENOPAUSE SYMPTOMS CHART

| TOO MUCH ESTROGEN | TOO LITTLE ESTROGEN |
| --- | --- |
| Bloating | Hot flashes |
| Tender, swelling breasts | Night sweats |
| Emotional problems: depression, hostility, irritability and mood swings | The same depression, hostility, irritability and mood swings that too much E causes |
| Weight gain | Problems sleeping |
| Decreased desire for sex | Anxiety |
| | A variety of cognitive problems, fuzzy brain and memory lapses |
| | Weight gain. |
| | Dry skin, vaginal dryness, vaginal itchiness or burning |
| | Thinning of her vaginal wall |
| | Painful intercourse as a result of the last two points |
| | A diminished sexual response and diminished sexual pleasure |
| | Vaginal or bladder infections |
| | Incontinence and urinary tract infections |
| | Migraines |

# APPENDIX 1

## *MORE ON ANDROPAUSE*

Here, as promised, is some additional information that wasn't included in the *Andropause: Men's Climate Change* Chapter.

### *ENVIRONMENTAL ESTROGEN*

We talked about how pervasive estrogen is in the environment, how you "ingest, inhale and absorb a constant drizzle of estrogenic chemicals through your skin", and how E builds up in your body. We didn't, however, tell you how you could decrease its impact. This checklist helps.

### *THE REDUCING ENVIRONMENTAL ESTROGENS CHECKLIST*

- Buy organic produce as much as possible.
- Buy hormone-free poultry, meat and pork.

- Use glass or ceramic containers to store your food.

- Buy plastics that don't use the industrial compounds PCB, BPA, or Phthalates. They usually say so on their labels.

- Use stainless steel water bottles.

- If you have to use a plastic container, don't heat it in the microwave or leave it in the sun.

- Use natural or organic skin care products.

- Use soaps, detergents and housecleaning products with fewer chemicals.

- Don't buy products with artificial scents.

- Don't use herbicides and only use natural pest control.

- Don't use condoms with spermicide for birth control.

- Buy low VOC, water-based paint.

- "Real men" use protective gear: use gloves and face masks when you work around paints, lacquers and solvents.

Check out the Environmental Working Group's data base on the relative toxicity of produce, sunscreens, household cleaning products and a variety of other goods at *www.ewg.org.*

## TESTING FOR TESTOSTERONE

You might have symptoms that point to Low T but are actually caused by other hormonal issues. Since your testes, adrenal glands and thyroid work together to maintain your hormonal balance, an imbalance in one impacts the other two;

high or low cortisol or high or low thyroid levels could be the real source of some of your symptoms. Therefore, both need to be checked out.

Your doctor will probably also want to look into other things, like your PSA for your prostate health.

## *THE MALE HORMONE TEST PANEL*

A complete blood count and chemistry profile that includes thyroid, liver-kidney function, glucose (sugar), minerals and lipids (fats).

- Cortisol
- *Pregnenolone*—a hormone that's the raw material for all other hormones, including testosterone, estrogen, progesterone and DHEA
- DHEA—a hormone that's converted into male and female hormones
- Total Estrogens
- Progesterone
- Total and Bioavailable Testosterone
- *Sex Binding Hormone Globulin*, which binds free testosterone, reducing the amount available to act on the tissues in your body. Unfortunately, as your T decreases in aging, SHBG increases
- PSA

Some doctors might also want to test one or more of these:

- *Estradiol*—(the enzyme aromatase converts T to estradiol)

- DHT—that high octane form of T we talked about in the *Being The Enforcer* section of *The Big T*

- *Luteinizing hormone* (LH)—a hormone that stimulates production of testosterone in men

As you can see, you want a complete check on everything that could be causing your Low T symptoms.

## *TESTOSTERONE REPLACEMENT OPTIONS*

If it turns out you do have Low T and need testosterone replacement therapy, there are a number of preparations to select from. You and your practitioner will have to weigh the cost, insurance coverage, convenience, ability to maintain stable T levels, and the side effects of the various formulations before deciding which is right for you. You also have a choice between pharmaceutical brands and getting your testosterone preparation custom-made at a compounding pharmacy. Here are the pros and cons of the most common TRT options.

---

*NOTE» EXCEPT FOR THE COMMERCIAL INJECTABLES, ALL THE FORMULATIONS ON OUR LIST ARE BIOIDENTICAL AND ARE SYNTHESIZED FROM SOY OR YAMS. THERE ARE, HOWEVER, SOME NEW SYNTHESIZED PRODUCTS, SO CHECK THE LABELS.*

---

# GELS (ANDROGEL, FORTESTA, TESTIM)

This is the most popular formulation and is easy to use. It comes in a clear gel, in single-use tubes, packets, or multiple-use pumps that deliver the amount your doctor prescribed. You rub it in once a day, usually in the morning, to your lower abdomen, arm or shoulder. It absorbs directly into your skin, which stores and releases it slowly into your bloodstream. This results in normal, stable T levels.

**CONS:** Since you don't want to wash it off, you need to wait two to six hours (depending on the brand) before showering, bathing or swimming.

Gels and the other transdermals, can also cause skin irritation, itching or blistering.

Since the gels and creams are absorbed through your skin, they are also absorbed through the skin of anyone who comes in contact with them. And they are potent. To get an idea, AndroGel dosages range from 20.25 mg-81mg. A woman getting TRT replacement normally uses 5-10 mgs. Imagine what they can do to someone who doesn't need any at all.

---

*WARNING» T GEL CAN HAVE HARMFUL EFFECTS ON PEOPLE, ESPECIALLY WOMEN OR CHILDREN, IF THEY TOUCH YOUR SKIN WHERE YOU APPLIED THE GEL, OR IF YOU HAVEN'T WASHED THE GEL OFF YOUR HANDS AND YOU TOUCH THEM.*

---

How harmful are the effects? The fetus of a pregnant woman could be damaged if she touches skin with gel on it. A woman could also find hair growing at new places on her body, or develop acne. Children might become aggressive or they could have sexual symptoms, such as enlarged genitals, pubic hair growth, feelings of sexual desire or increased desire. Boys might get more erections. Although these symptoms usually disappear once they stop having contact with the T gel, kids' genitals can sometimes continue to be abnormally large. T gel can also make their bones mature too rapidly, so they stop growing earlier than they should and don't reach their expected heights. Plus, their bones can continue to be too mature even after they stop having contact with the T gel.

---

***WARNING***» *ALWAYS WASH YOUR HANDS THOROUGHLY WITH SOAP AND WATER AFTER APPLYING THE T GEL.*

---

If you expect to have skin-to-skin contact with someone, wash the area. Or if someone accidentally touches a gel-covered area, make sure he or she scrupulously washes the area with soap and water.

You also need to alert others who are handling anything that could have T gel on it to be very careful. Estimated Price: $230-$500 a month.

## COMPOUNDED GELS OR CREAMS

These are used in the same way, but you can get a prescription for the exact strength you need. Also, less is more: you get higher concentrations of T packed into smaller amounts of gel or cream. Moreover, there's less irritation than you get with the patch, and they are much cheaper than AndroGel, Fortesta and Testim.

**CONS:** While some men find the compounded formulations to be more effective than the pharmaceuticals, others find it doesn't absorb into their skin very well, so their symptoms don't get handled. The potential of the undesirable transferal of T to family or pets also remains an issue. Estimated Price: $30-$100 a month.

## SKIN PATCH (ANDRODERM)

A skin patch is also a transdermal that is applied once daily, but usually at night. You wear it on your arm, upper body, back, thigh or scrotum. Again, it enables you to maintain a stable amount of T throughout a 24-hour period.

**CONS:** The patch has a higher possibility of skin issues than the gel. It rarely reaches the optimal level of T and can fall off when you perspire. The patch is large and the adhesive strong, so when you pull it off you can get a skin burn and welts. It needs to be put on a hairless spot, and so you might have to shave that area first. You must also be careful not to put it on an oily or sweaty spot, on a shoulder or hipbone, on a cut, wound, or irritated area, and it needs to lie flat during normal activity. You also have to rotate where you put it, waiting seven days before using the same spot again.

---

**WARNING**» *THROW USED PATCHES AWAY IN A TRASHCAN THAT KIDS AND PETS CAN'T OPEN OR REACH. IT CAN BE DANGEROUS FOR THEM TO CHEW ON OR PLAY WITH USED T PATCHES.*

---

Estimated Price: $240-$500 a month.

## COMPOUNDED PATCHES

They have same pros and cons, except that the dose is individualized for the patient. The adhesive might not cause skin irritation.

## MOUTH PATCH (STRIANT)

You apply a tablet-shaped mouth patch to your upper gum every 12 hours. It rapidly releases the T into your bloodstream, and provides steady delivery.

**CONS:** Although you can brush your teeth, eat, and drink, the patch could fall off. Furthermore, you could swallow it. There also can be side effects that are specific to your mouth such as gum irritation, tenderness, pain, swelling, blistering, stinging lips, trouble tasting food or the food tasting bad or bitter, or toothache.

Estimated Price: $250 a month.

# INJECTABLES (DEPO-TESOSTERONE, DELATESTRYL)

These formulations are injected into your muscles every 7-22 days and are the least expensive of your options.

**CONS:** They are painful. The T levels also vary, reaching their highest levels two to three days after the injection, then slowly decreasing until you get the next one. You therefore get fluctuations in the relief of your symptoms: you can feel over stimulated right after the shot, just right, then tired and have a low sex drive. Giving yourself injections weekly may help. On the other hand, the injection sites can become infected.

Since the medicine has to be refrigerated, it can be a hassle if you're traveling. Besides, you might feel awkward explaining to the TSA personnel why you've packed a syringe and a controlled medicine.

They are not bioidentical.

Estimated Price: $30-$150 a month, depending on if you or your partner injects you or a doctor or nurse does the injection.

# COMPOUNDED INJECTABLES

They have the same pros and cons, except that the dose is individualized so you get the exact amount of T you need. They are also bioidentical.

Estimated Price: $88-$177, depending on the strength and quantity and if you buy it from a compounding pharmacy. The price can be much higher if you get it at a clinic.

## IMPLANTS (TESTOPOL)

This involves implanting eight to ten 75 mg. T pellets under the skin of your buttocks or hip area, which slowly release over three to four months. Then you need to repeat the process. Implants are considered exceptionally effective, easy, and convenient because you don't have to use something every day and they maintain a consistent level. The dose can be adjusted up or down by adding or subtracting pellets. Many men who need higher levels of T prefer implants because they handle their Low T symptoms better than gels and creams—particularly in the areas of energy and sexual performance. There also isn't the risk of exposing your partner, kids or pets to testosterone.

**CONS:** It's hard to predict the right dosage, so you might have to endure having too much or too little for three to four months before you figure it out. Needing a minor surgical procedure three to four times a year can be a hassle. You might also be bruised or sore for a few days to a week after it. Although it's infrequent, the pellets can push out. Even more rarely, you can get an infection from the surgery.

Estimated Price: $80 per pellet. The cost of insertion varies by clinic.

## COMPOUNDED PELLETS

The pros and cons are basically the same, except that the compounded pellets last from four to six months. Depending on the size and number used, it can also be cheaper. Estimated Price: $40-$75 per pellet. The cost of insertion varies by clinic.

## COMPOUNDED LOZENGES OR DROPS

As mentioned in the Andropause Chapter, T pills are a lose-lose form of TRT: they go through the liver, are ineffective and may increase liver toxicity and the risk of liver cancer. Testosterone lozenges, however, are another story. Dissolved under your tongue or between your cheek and gum one to four times a day, they are absorbed directly into your bloodstream. They quickly increase your T to the best range to handle your symptoms. Compounding pharmacies can also add flavors to mitigate the bitterness of T you can get from a mouth patch.

**CONS:** Lozenges rapidly raise your T levels, which can then lower and fluctuate. That sudden rise can also increase your estradiol more than other T delivery systems. Men with liver problems shouldn't take them because they may swallow some T.

Estimated Price: $30-$100 a month.

# APPENDIX 2

## *WEATHER PROTECTION FOR WOMEN*

You may wonder why there is an entire appendix on Hormone Replacement Therapy. The short answer is that after people read all about the perimenopausal and postmenopausal symptoms and problems in *Menopause: Women's Climate Change*, they told us they needed to know how to fix them. We knew Hormone Replacement Therapy (HRT, for short and for the rest of the appendix) is the best, most effective way. Fine, we thought, we'll write a few pages. Then we started the research, went through a phase of complete confusion, and many months and 32 pages later, we added this appendix to cover the scope of what we learned. So consider this section a bonus, our gift to you.

As you will see, it differs from the rest of the book because, sadly, there are no jokes, and there's no attempt to use fighter pilot analogies.

## WHO NEEDS TO READ THIS?

This chapter speaks to women who are suffering from perimenopausal or postmenopausal symptoms, and are either considering hormone replacement therapy or are already on it. Knowledge is not only power, it's also peace of mind. Are you a guy who doesn't want to sit hopelessly by while your partner can't sleep, goes through mood swings or loses her sex drive? If you want to help both her, and your relationship, you need this data. Of course it's up to your mate to decide what's best for her own body, but you can still be an educated sounding board. She'll love you for it.

## THE HORMONE REPLACEMENT THERAPY (HRT) BRIEFING

As of this writing, HRT is the most effective treatment for the symptoms of perimenopause and postmenopause. Your partner's decision whether or not to use it may be the biggest decision she makes in climate change. Why don't all women who need it, use it? Because there's a lot of fear caused by confusion, controversy, incomplete information, misinformation, and lack of scientific study and agreement. In order to make an informed decision, your mate needs to weigh her physical and mental distress against her anxiety about HRT's possible risks. Here's some basic information to help her and you, to navigate through the haze.

## WHO USES IT?

The FDA recommends Hormone Replacement Therapy to reduce hot flashes, night sweats, vaginal dryness and bone loss in osteoporosis. Women also use HRT Jbecause they want a vibrant sex life, moist skin, clearer thinking, better moods—in other words, help with all the symptoms of perimenopause. Many stop once their wild up-and-down hormonal imbalances abate in postmenopause. At that point, their hot flashes, night sweats, mood swings, crankiness and foggy brains are greatly reduced or completely eliminated. (But not dry skin, dry vaginas, some cognitive problems and low libido.) Others never stop using it because they still have troubling symptoms or they refuse to give up their quality of life. Smaller groups begin once their periods have ended or to handle their symptoms or health issues, like osteoporosis, osteoarthritis, and although the FDA no longer recommends it, heart disease.

## WHAT HORMONES ARE REPLACED?

As you might guess, everybody gets estrogen. Women with a uterus must also take progesterone to protect them from uterine (endometrial) cancer.

---

*NOTE»* *E REPLACEMENT CAN CAUSE TOO*
*MUCH CELL GROWTH OF THE UTERINE LINING*
*(ENDOMETRIUM). PROGESTERONE STOPS*
*THAT EFFECT.*

---

Since women who have had a hysterectomy don't have a uterus, they don't have to take progesterone to prevent that cell growth. There are doctors, however, who prescribe it anyway because of its many other health benefits.

Some physicians also give women testosterone to boost their sex drive, but that's not what's usually meant when you see HRT. It's called *TRT— testosterone replacement therapy.* We'll take a look at that after we review what we know about HRT.

## WHY ARE WOMEN AFRAID?

Once upon a time, HRT had a great reputation, not only as a solution to women's peri and postmenopausal symptoms, but also as an anti-aging protector against bone fracture, heart disease and dementia. Wyeth manufactured two products that were and still are the most prescribed HRT used in the United States. *Premarin* is an estrogen only pill, and *Prempro* is a combination estrogen and *progestin* pill.

---

*NOTE»* *PROGESTIN IS THE GENERIC NAME*
*FOR SYNTHETIC PROGESTERONE.*

---

Wyeth had so much confidence in their products that they successfully campaigned to have them used exclusively in the National Institutes of Health Women's Initiative (WHI) of 27,347 women. The vast majority of their subjects were postmenopausal. Half took the HRT and the other half took placebos. Then Boom! In 2002, the trial of Wyeth's combined estrogen+progestin pill (16,680 women) was stopped after five and a half years because there was a statistically significant increase in invasive breast cancer, coronary heart disease, strokes and blood clot rates. Hip fractures and colorectal cancer rates, however, decreased. See for yourself: here are the numbers, per every 10,000 women:

| | WITHOUT HRT | WITH HRT |
|---|---|---|
| Blood clots | 16 | 34 |
| Breast Cancer | 30 | 38 |
| Colorectal Cancer | 16 | 10 |
| Endometrial Cancer | 6 | 5 |
| Heart Attacks | 30 | 37 |
| Hip Fractures | 15 | 10 |
| Strokes | 21 | 29 |
| Deaths | 53 | 52 |

In February 2004, the trial of Wyeth's estrogen-only formula (10,667 women) was also brought to an abrupt end because, while there was a 23% decrease in breast cancer, heart attacks and strokes increased.

Now you can see why women and their doctors got frightened. HRT's popularity nose-dived, and prescriptions for Wyeth's hormone products fell by 50%. Since that time, there has been a sharp and stable drop in breast cancer rates.

---

**NOTE»** *WHEN THE WOMEN STOPPED THEIR HRT, THEIR SYMPTOMS RETURNED.*

---

## MORE BAD NEWS

In 2003, another bomb exploded. This time it was in the UK where 1.3 million British women, ages 50-64 were enrolled from 1996-2001 in the Million Women Study. Half used various formulas of HRT, including Wyeth's, and half didn't use anything. Both groups filled out questionnaires aimed at determining the effects of HRT on breast cancer. The results found that estrogen+progestin users had twice the risk of breast cancer and more fatal breast cancer. Estrogen-only users had a slightly higher risk. As in the States, HRT use dramatically declined.

## JUDGING RESULTS

Given that every woman goes through climate change and many of them need help, you'd think that there would be an abundance of HRT research. Wrong. Actually, there are only a handful of double-blind trials and big observational studies. And there haven't been enough smaller studies that test a variety of products, doses or means of delivery to come up with definitive answers. That's one reason why the reports from both sides of the Atlantic had such a big impact on how all HRT is viewed: in the absence of much information, people rely on the little they have.

There are many different hormonal products on the market here in the US. But because Wyeth's are the oldest and most widely used, the majority of US research employs their ingredients.

When you read about the results of HRT studies, big and small, you're usually reading about what happens to women who use Wyeth's proprietary formulas.

## WYETH'S FORMULA

So what did Wyeth (and now Pfizer, who bought them in 2009) use? To begin with, you need to know that women naturally create progesterone and three kinds of estrogen which all have specific chemical and molecular structures. They are, in order of their strength, estradiol, estrone and estriol. The Wyeth formula doesn't use any of these: it takes E extracted from pregnant horse urine (*Premarin*—pregnant mare urine) for its estrogen-only formula and adds a progestin—*medroxy-progesterone acetate or MAP*—for its combined product (*Prempro*). "Why?" you may wonder. Because you can't get a patent on natural substances. You have to change them.

Wyeth's biggest competitor is bioidentical hormones, which do have the exact same chemical and molecular structure as your mate's body uses. But more about them later.

Getting back to the Women's Health Initiative. Since it became the standard for many people for the benefits and dangers of all HRT, no matter the formula, you need to factor in the strength, means of delivery, and age of recipients employed: equine estrogen is much stronger than your mate's natural E and they administered their most potent dose in a pill to primarily postmenopausal women. You'll see why that matters in the next few pages.

## WHAT DID THE U.S. FOOD AND DRUG ADMINISTRATION DO?

When the results of the Women's Health Initiative were published, the FDA acted. The FDA doesn't guarantee safety. It weighs the benefits vs. the risks of a medicine, and in this case determined that Wyeth's products did more good than harm. It, however, recognized the dangers and:

1. Assumed that all HRT products, whatever their ingredients, dose or means of delivery, carried the same risks as Premarin, Prempro and Provera (the Wyeth progestin).

2. Required FDA-approved HRT to carry a "black box," warning that HRT could increase some women's risk of "blood clots, heart attacks, strokes, breast cancer, and gall bladder disease".

3. Recommended using the lowest dose for the shortest
   time to ease symptoms.

## CONTROVERSY AND CONFUSION

While many people think using the lowest dose for the shortest time to handle symptoms sounds practical enough, numerous health professionals don't agree with the sweeping generality that all HRT carries the same risks for everybody. A body of evidence is slowly growing that suggests they're right.

## DOES AGE MATTER?

Yes. Nowadays there's a general consensus that the sooner your mate starts HRT, the safer it is.

But before we get into how that was decided, a reminder: all the info and conclusions here refer to Wyeth's ingredients—*conjugated equine estrogen (CEE)* and *medroxy-progesterone acetate (MAP).* We'll just call them CEE and MAP from now on.

Researchers tend to keep analyzing results of trials and studies, and so the Women's Health Initiative was reexamined. What became clear was that of most of the women in the trial were postmenopausal, had an average age of 63.5, and had started HRT ten years after their periods stopped. That's a very specific group. Only 5000 of the 27,347 women were perimenopausal and they had a much better risks-benefits ratio.

---

***NOTE*»** *WOMEN BETWEEN THE AGES 50-55*
*HAD LESS HEART DISEASE AND DEATH FROM*
*ANY CAUSE THAN THE PLACEBO GROUP.*

---

Additional research since 2004 confirms those findings for the 50-59 group:

- Heart scans revealed 60% lower risk of severe coronary artery calcium, which predicts heart disease.

- Another randomized controlled trial revealed a lower risk of heart attack.

- There's evidence of some protection against lung cancer.

- There's no increase in breast cancer rates for short-term, 2-3 year use to alleviate symptoms.

Did your partner have a hysterectomy? After re-analyzing the WHI data, it turns out that *women without a uterus benefited more than women with one*! Aside from less breast cancer and heart protection, there were no new breast cancers after seven years. Actually, there was *less* danger of getting invasive breast cancer.

How about starting menopause before 40? Today the thought is that if there's no history of breast cancer risk, a woman can safely take HRT until she's 51; the average age of climate change. The same holds for women who've had hysterectomies.

***WARNING*»** *RESEARCHERS FOUND A 32%*
*HIGHER RISK OF STROKE IN CEE+MAP*
*USERS—NO MATTER HOW OLD THEY WERE OR*
*WHEN THEY STARTED USE.*

A conflicting study agreed that stroke risk increased with CEE+MAP, but not when they used a different type of engineered estrogen. Therefore, that alarming statistic may really only be for CEE+MAP.

The bottom line is that gynecologists generally agree it's pretty safe for younger women to use HRT to relieve menopausal symptoms.

***NOTE*»** *IT'S BEST TO START AS SOON AS*
*THE SYMPTOMS REAR THEIR UGLY HEADS*
*AND FOLLOW "THE LOWEST DOSE FOR THE*
*SHORTEST TIME" RULE.*

## POSTMENOPAUSE

What if your lover is one of those women who start the treatment close to menopause and never stop because of her symptoms or because she wants help with her bones, or sex life? It's hard to say since the research hasn't been done yet.

What if a woman wants to start after her periods stop? That's where we do have some answers.

Doctors prescribe HRT to women after menopause, because when their estrogen declines, osteoporosis (thinning bones), cardiac heart disease, breast cancer, memory loss and dementia increase. Does HRT help?

Osteoporosis definitely gets a thumb up. The Women's Health Initiative confirmed what has universally been found: HRT increases bone mineral density, halting or slowing bone loss.

---

**NOTE**» USING E PLUS, A CALCIUM SUPPLEMENT, IS TWICE AS EFFECTIVE AS ONLY USING E.

---

The WHI and other studies also found that there were fewer colorectal or cancers of the endometrium (lining of the womb).

---

**NOTE**» FATTER WOMEN HAD BETTER PROTECTION FROM ENDOMETRIAL CANCER.

---

So much for the benefits. Now for the risks.

All the scary Women's Health Initiative data came from postmenopausal women who started Premarin or Prempro *at least ten years after their cycles stopped*.

HRT decreases bad cholesterol (LDL) and increases healthy cholesterol (HDL). Since heart attacks are the number one killer of postmenopausal women, and a high level of HDL is believed to protect against heart attacks, the hope was that HRT would help.

With this in mind, Wyeth funded a large randomized trial using Prempro for postmenopausal women who already had heart disease. It did indeed increase HDL by 10% and reduce LDL by 11%, but the rate of further heart attacks or deaths from coronary heart disease stayed the same. Blood clots in the lungs and veins increased.

A few years later, the WHI found an increase in heart attacks, strokes, and blood clots in the veins and arteries. So much for heart protection from the Wyeth products.

Other unwelcome confirmation of WHI findings came from studies here and abroad and included other chemically altered brands; they concluded that postmenopausal women using HRT were more likely to develop breast cancer than those who never used it.

---

**WARNING»** *IF YOUR LOVER HAS A HISTORY OF SMOKING, STARTING HRT AFTER MENOPAUSE CAN PROMOTE THE GROWTH OF LUNG CANCERS.*

---

A lot of women find that HRT is a big help with their cognitive and memory problems. But that doesn't seem to translate into guarding against dementia: most studies don't find it has any effect at all and one showed an increase in dementia.

The bottom line in terms of age and Premarin and Prempro: the pros of a particular woman may outweigh the cons, but the older she gets and the longer it has been since her last period, the riskier it is.

Now that you have a brain full of facts about HRT, it's time to add more info about the other alternatives. Fortunately, there are many.

## WHAT ARE THE OTHER OPTIONS?

The good thing about medicines approved by the Food and Drug Administration is that you know what's in them. Whether or not you like their ingredients, they meet the rigorous *USP (United States Pharmacopeia)* standards for quality, strength and consistency for over-the-counter and prescriptions drugs.

One category of FDA-approved HRT concerns the ones that can be patented because they're chemically altered or are completely synthetic. They currently include: nine estrogen, three progestin, and two combined E+progestin brands.

They also approve many brands in that other category we mentioned earlier—bioidentical hormones.

## WHAT ARE BIOIDENTICAL HORMONES?

*Bioidentical hormones* are extracted from plants and prepared in labs to have exactly the same chemical and molecular structure as the hormones our bodies produce. Usually, estrogen is made from soy and wild yams. Progesterone is made from wild yams and is *finely ground (micronized)* so that it can be absorbed better. Testosterone can come from either. In case you were wondering, Mother Nature owns the patent to bioidenticals.

---

**NOTE**» *CHOWING DOWN YAMS AT DINNER WON'T HELP. WILD YAMS ARE A DIFFERENT SPECIES.*

---

**CAUTION**» *OVER-THE-COUNTER PROGESTERONE CREAMS MAY BE TOO WEAK TO BE EFFECTIVE AND THE BODY DOESN'T CONVERT YAM EXTRACT CREAMS INTO \PROGESTERONE.*

---

There are, however, over-the-counter brands that are already converted from wild yam into progesterone. Check the label to make sure that progesterone, not wild yams, is listed on the supplement facts.

## WHAT ARE THE BIOIDENTICAL OPTIONS?

Your mate can either get an FDA-approved brand or she can have her hormones custom-made for her at a compounding pharmacy. What's the difference?

FDA-approved bioidenticals:

- Are micronized and come in standard doses, usually two strengths

- Only use estradiol, the strongest estrogen

- Are currently available in 13 different brands of estradiol

- Come in a patch, tablet, capsule, lozenge, sublingual drops, gel, vaginal cream, vaginal insert, vaginal

301

tablet, suppository, skin cream and spray, depending on the brand

- Only have one brand of progesterone, which comes in a capsule

- Are available in 5 different estrogen+progestin products, none of which are totally bioidentical: they all use estradiol, but the progesterone is chemically modified, so it has a different chemical structure from the one produced by a woman's body

FDA-approved bioidenticals work fine for a lot of women, but not for all. What if a woman needs a different strength? Or a doctor thinks that some forms of hormones or delivery are safer and better? In that case they can customize her bioidentical hormone replacement (from now on BHRT). A growing number of physicians are writing prescriptions to compounding pharmacies where they can:

- Use any of the three forms of estrogen—estradiol, estrone or estriol, or combine them

- Use micronized progesterone

- Use testosterone, which isn't approved for women in either HRT or BHRT by the FDA

- Adjust the strength of the dose to fit the woman

- Use any means of delivery they think is best for each hormone

---

***NOTE***» *THE FDA ONLY DEALS WITH DRUG COMPANIES AND ENSURES THEIR STANDARDS THROUGH THE FDA'S DRUG APPROVAL PROCESS. THEY DON'T OVERSEE COMPOUNDED PHARMACIES, WHOSE PRODUCTS ARE PRESCRIBED BY A PHYSICIAN AND MADE ON A PATIENT-TO-PATIENT BASIS.*

---

Since compounding pharmacies don't report to the FDA, no one knows how many women are using compounded bioidenticals.

## THE BHRT BRIEFING

After the Women's Health Initiative results were published, a lot of women didn't stop taking hormones. They migrated over to BHRT. Since that time, there's also been a growing trend in the US to use more natural products and alternative medicine either as a primary or supplemental form of healing. And more and more gynecologists either prefer BHRT or at least offer it as an option along with HRT. But not everyone agrees BHRT is the way to go.

## HORMONE WARS

HRT vs. BHRT. If you do an Internet search, you'll find numerous articles written by prominent doctors and researchers with strong, opposing viewpoints. BHRT supporters are convinced that it is much more beneficial than HRT and poses way fewer risks. The HRT camp is adamant that BHRT is no better and makes unproven claims. It can be very confusing and difficult to sort out the data. We know, because it took us a while to figure out why physicians and patients choose one over the other.

Here's what we came up with. We're going to start with HRT advocates because that gives you a basis of comparison.

## WHY DO MANY DOCTORS PREFER HRT?

1. MDs aren't generally taught to think "natural," or to use compounding pharmacies. They're trained to use prescription, FDA-approved drugs with standard doses.

2. Everything they recommend has side effects and risks and they consider, as does the FDA and many health organizations, that the advantages of HRT far outweigh the dangers.

3. They also believe that our bodies handle all hormones, whether they have the identical chemistry or not, exactly the same way; therefore HRT and BHRT have exactly the same risks and benefits. So, why not use established, tested products such as Premarin, Provera, and Prempro?

4. Doctors are overwhelmingly busy and often get their information from medical journals containing articles that are ghostwritten by Wyeth-Pfizer's marketing department. Forty-four of these articles came to light in 2009 as a result of a lawsuit brought by 8000 women who alleged that Prempro caused their breast

cancers. Usually Wyeth-Pfizer paid some academic professor at a prestigious university medical center to use his or her name, and then wrote their own piece. You can guess the slant: they minimized the unfavorable effects of their products and created uncertainty about their main rival—bioidentical hormones.

5. They dismiss or are skeptical of data that doesn't come from a double-blind, American-run trial. Until now, there haven't been any for bioidenticals because drug companies didn't see any financial benefit if they couldn't get a patent.

But that's changing! The National Institute on Aging is sponsoring a five-year clinical trial of 643 women divided into two groups: those within six years of menopause and those 10+ years past it. Half will get *Estrace*, the number one bioidentical FDA-approved brand of estradiol, and those with a uterus will also get a micronized progesterone gel. The other half will use placebos. The results are expected in 2014. We don't know about you, but we can't wait to see the outcome. Stay tuned.

## WHY DO SOME DOCTORS PREFER BIOIDENTICALS?

Physicians who prescribe bioidenticals strongly believe that hormones with the exact chemical and molecular structure as those created by the body are better and safer than chemically engineered hormones. Why? Here are some reasons:

1. *All* kinds of estrogens can lock onto the E receptors in your mate's body, but they differ in terms of how useful they are and how they affect individual tissues.

2. For instance, take the estrogens your lover makes: a very small amount of potent estradiol circulating in the blood causes powerful changes in your mate's tissue when it locks on to E receptors. Estrone less so, and estriol much less so. That means there is a difference in what estrogen you use. Ditto progesterone.

3. Bioidentical hormones help molecules break down and process identical hormones. This minimizes side effects, which can be a problem with altered hormones.

4. Your mate's body, on the other hand, has to figure out what to do and how to break down and process pregnant horse urine or a synthetic estrogen or progesterone.

## WHAT DO STUDIES SHOW?

Another big difference is that bioidentical proponents think that observational and communal health studies are valid. And they don't care which country it comes from. That's fortunate because so much of the data we have on BHRT comes from Europe, where women and their health systems have been confidently using bioidenticals for more than half a century.

France, which has socialized medicine, overwhelmingly prescribes bioidenticals to treat peri and postmenopause. There, 83% of women use a transdermal estradiol gel and 58% use oral micronized progesterone. Only 3% use medroxyprogesterone acetate (MAP), which is the progestin in Wyeth's Prempro. A study, led by Agnes Fournier (hence called the Fournier study) compared 54,548 postmenopausal hormone users and non-users to see the effects of BHRT and HRT. In 2005, after five years of follow-up, they concluded "there was no significant increase in breast cancer" for the bioidentical group.

---

*WARNING» THOSE WHO USED ESTRADIAL+MAP HAD A 40% INCREASED RISK.*

---

Three years later, with eight years of follow up, they found no difference in breast cancer risk between women who used BHRT and women who didn't use anything.

---

*WARNING» THOSE USING SYNTHETIC PROGESTERONE HAD A 69% HIGHER RISK OF DEVELOPING BREAST CANCER.*

---

More damning evidence re: breast cancer and artificial progesterone can be found in studies published in prestigious, peer-reviewed international medical journals, such as *Climacteric* and *Maturitas*, which specialize in andropause and menopause.

Earlier in 2002, the de Ligniere's study published in *Climateric* also reported that, while using bioidenticals didn't increase breast cancer, using synthetic progesterone did.

A medical literature review in *Maturitas* concurred. It went further to suggest that using transdermal (through the skin) estrogens and natural progesterone "might offer significant benefits and added safety." It also pointed to evidence that found that natural progesterone "displays a favorable action on the vessels and the brain."

"A favorable action" on the vessels is important because strokes and heart disease are two other risks that are increased when artificial progesterone is combined with estrogen.

## MORE WEATHER TRIALS

Happily, there is an increasing number of United States researchers doing small studies of BHT.

Does your lover have heart problems? 56 postmenopausal women with angina pectoris (chest pains) were given estradiol and *drospirenone* (another synthetic progesterone) for 6 weeks. Chest pains mean there's less blood and therefore less oxygen flowing to the heart muscle. Too little oxygen and you have a heart attack. The results were hopeful for the estradiol women. While more blood and oxygen went to their heart muscles, less went to the hearts of the placebo group.

---

**NOTE**» *SEVERAL STUDIES ALSO REPORTED THAT THIS SAME COMBINATION LOWERED BLOOD PRESSURE.*

---

Back to her heart. Other cardiac studies showed that women getting estradiol, but not the placebo groups, had reduced levels of a substance from a cell that constricts blood vessels and which is partly to blame for heart attacks.

Does your lover have osteoporosis? We already know estradiol is recommended for building bones, but could an ultralow dose still prevent bone loss and be safer?

Yes. A little goes a long way, as proved by a three-year trial using .025 mg of micronized estradiol a day, which is one-quarter of the normal dose. A group of 83 women, 65+, were treated with estradiol while 84 women received a placebo. Ladies who didn't have a hysterectomy also got 100mg. micronized progesterone a day. Team estradiol increased their bone mineral density by 2.6% in the neck of the hip, 3.6% in the total hip, 2.8% in the spine, and 1.2% in the whole body. Team placebo didn't show an increase. Plus there were minimal side effects and no breast cancer in either group.

A later study backed them up, this time by comparing *raloxifene,* a leading osteoporosis drug. Some women can't or don't want the medicine because of its worrisome side effects. Five-hundred women were given either a tiny 0.14 mg dose of estradiol a day or 60 mg of raloxifene. At the end of two years, 77% of the estradiol ladies showed no bone loss in their lumbar spine and had a 2.4% increase in bone mineral density. Of their raloxifene sisters 80.5 % didn't lose any bone in the same area and added on 3% bone mineral density. Again, no breast cancer was found.

These kinds of tests are encouraging, aren't they? We just need more.

## WHAT'S THE SAFEST DELIVERY SYSTEM?

When it comes to strokes, bioidenticals and means of delivery make a difference. If you take a hormone pill, it goes through your liver and is modified before it's absorbed, which increases your risks. Researchers found that oral, chemically altered estrogen potentially stimulates the production of blood-clotting proteins. But bioidentical E that goes directly through your skin in a spray, cream, gel or a suppository doesn't produce those proteins or increase your risk of having a stroke.

---

***NOTE*** *» MICRONIZED ESTRADIOL IN A PILL FORM IS CONVERTED TO ESTRONE, WHICH IS THE E THAT WOMEN PRODUCE THE MOST OF DURING AND AFTER MENOPAUSE.*

---

An earlier study, this time in Denmark, looked at hormones and heart attacks. There, bioidentical estradiol and another progestin (*norethindrone acetate*, which is also FDA-approved) are the hormones of choice. After following 700,000 women for six years, the investigators didn't find a direct connection between hormone therapy and heart attacks. The only blip was that they did see an increase of heart attacks in younger users, but they pointed out that using transdermals lowered that risk.

As information accumulates about the different modes of delivery, the "better safe than sorry" school is shifting to bioidenticals and from pills to products that go directly into the blood stream.

## WHAT DO STUDIES ON COMPOUNDED BHRT SHOW?

Trick question. There aren't any. You need to extrapolate the data from the other BHRT studies. But since compounded formulas have different strengths, means of delivery, and combinations of E, they're not the same as those used in the studies.

## IS THERE A DIFFERENCE IN HOW DOCTORS DECIDE ON THE DOSE?

Another point of contention between HRT and BHRT practitioners is the use of blood tests. Doctors who prescribe bioidenticals take them to determine what the hormone levels are and what dose to prescribe. Why?

1. They can. Women have normal levels of their own hormones, so there is a base of comparison.
2. They believe that imbalanced hormones cause symptoms and other problems, so they want to make

sure the hormones are balanced.

3. They want to make sure nothing else is going on that needs to be addressed.

Non-bioidentical hormone supporters think blood tests aren't necessary and don't do them because:

1. They can't. Women don't produce equine estrogen or synthetic hormones, so there are no "normal" levels to serve as a base of comparison.

2. They think it's a total waste. They're treating for symptom relief, not balance, and as far as they're concerned, HRT handles the symptoms.

---

***WARNING***» *SOME PRACTITIONERS USE SALIVA TESTS, BUT THEY'RE NOT ACCURATE. BLOOD TESTS ARE.*

---

Okay, so now you know why many doctors and women choose bioidenticals. The next big question is:

## WHICH IS BETTER? FDA-APPROVED OR COMPOUNDED BIOIDENTICALS?

A lot of doctors prescribe both, depending on the needs of the woman. Others may prefer one to the other. Just to clarify the pros and cons of each, here's a list. We know we've pointed out some of this before, but given that you've just read a whole bunch of information, it may bear repeating.

## WHY DO DOCTORS AND WOMEN CHOOSE FDA-APPROVED BIOIDENTICALS?

- They're sure of the quality and strength of the bioidenticals.

- They want to use estradiol because that's what a woman produces in her ovaries during her fertile years.

- Estradiol comes in every imaginable mode of delivery.

- They don't think women need tailor-made doses. One of the two available strengths usually works fine.

- They think oral micronized progesterone is as safe as transdermal progesterone.

- If they use the combined product, they don't think the artificial progesterone is harmful.

- Insurance companies that pay for hormone therapy will pay for it.

---

**NOTE**» *INSURANCE COMPANIES MAY NOT PAY FOR COMPOUNDED PRODUCTS.*

---

## WHY DO DOCTORS AND WOMEN CHOOSE COMPOUNDED FORMULAS?

- Compounding pharmacies use the same, micronized ingredients as the FDA-approved products, so they're equally pure.

So THAT'S Why They Do That

- They trust the compounding pharmacies they have a relationship with to deliver the correct quality and dose.

---

**WARNING**» *ONLY USE A PHARMACY, ESPECIALLY ON-LINE, THAT THE DOCTOR RECOMMENDS AND IS LISTED ON WWW.PCAB. ORG/, THE WEBSITE OF THE PHARMACEUTICAL COMPOUNDING ACCREDITATION BOARD.*

---

- They think oral progesterone is not as safe and want to use a transdermal progesterone.

- They want to use testosterone– usually in a transdermal.

- They want to control the dose to fit the woman and they want the flexibility to change it over time as conditions or needs change.

- They believe that estriol, the weakest estrogen, which is not FDA-approved, is the safest to use.

- They usually mix the estrogens. Sometimes they use all three—80% estriol, 10% estrone and 10% estradiol. Most often they use 80% estriol and 20% estradiol, but will increase the estradiol if they need a stronger blend to handle the symptoms.

A word on estriol: many small trials have proven that it is just as effective as other forms of E in relieving menopausal symptoms. Some doctors believe it protects against breast cancer because women who have higher estriol levels in relation to their estrone and estradiol levels have lower breast

314

cancer rates. A Japanese study showed it lowered triglyceride and cholesterol levels while increasing the healthy cholesterol in women 70-84, but not 50-65.

## HOT OFF THE PRESS –2012 RESULTS COMPARING HRT AND BHRT

Finally, we have a comparison of CEE and bioidentical estradiol and progesterone in one study. The results, we are overjoyed to report, are really encouraging for women who start hormone replacement within three years after their menopausal symptoms start.

We can thank the non-profit Kronos Longevity Research Institute for this four-year, double blind, placebo-controlled clinical trial of 727 women aged 42-58 (52 on average.) Get familiar with its acronym, KEEPS (Kronos Early Estrogen Prevention Study) because it's the first of its kind and probably will be referred to in newspaper and Internet articles for a long time to come.

What KEEPS did was divide the women into three groups receiving: the placebo; CEE (Premarin); and a transdermal estradiol patch (*Climera*, 50 ug/day).

---

**NOTE**» *THE ORAL PREMARIN WAS AT A MUCH LOWER DOSE THAN THE ONE USED IN THE WOMEN'S HEALTH INITIATIVE—0.45MG/DAY VS. 0.625 MG/DAY.*

---

Another significant difference is that KEEPS didn't use synthetic progesterone with either the CEE or estradiol. Both groups got oral micronized progesterone (*Prometrium*) for 12 days every month.

## HOW EFFECTIVE WERE BOTH TYPES OF E?

To quote its authors," The data showed improvements in cognition, mood, menopausal symptoms, and sexual function in younger women." By menopausal symptoms, they mean hot flashes, night sweats, dry vagina, and bone density.

However, if sex is an issue, your lover should get the patch. The women in both groups had more lubrication and less pain, but only the women using bioidentical estradiol had more desire and arousal.

## HOW SAFE WERE BOTH TYPES OF E?

Very. KEEPS didn't find any negative effects on breast cancer, endometrial cancer, blood pressure, blood clots, heart attacks, or strokes. It did acknowledge, however, that a much larger trial was needed to draw definitive conclusions.

There were some differences between the two forms of estrogen.

---

**NOTE**» *ONLY THE CEE RAISED THE HEALTHY
CHOLESTEROL AND REDUCED THE BAD.
BUT IT ALONE ALSO RAISED THE AMOUNT
OF TRIGLYCERIDES, A TYPE OF FAT IN OUR
BLOOD THAT WE USE FOR ENERGY. HIGH
TRIGLYCERIDES INCREASE OUR RISK FOR
HEART DISEASE.*

---

**NOTE**» *ONLY THE ESTRADIOL LOWERED
INSULIN RESISTANCE.*

---

In case you don't know what that means, we'll explain. Insulin controls the breakdown of sugars, starches and fats in our body. When our cells resist insulin, our body has to produce more. Too much insulin can lead to diabetes and other illnesses. So lowered insulin resistance is a good thing.

It's nice to leave this section on an encouraging note. Now on to testosterone.

## TESTOSTERONE REPLACEMENT THERAPY (TRT)

Talking about testosterone, here at last, for you sex-starved couples, is some information on replacing it.

As mentioned, the FDA doesn't approve any testosterone formula for women. On the other hand, the FDA does approve bioidentical brands of T for men with low testosterone levels. Six of the bioidenticals come in very high standard dose gels, so maybe a doctor could prescribe one of them. But how do you cut it down to the right dose for a woman? It's easier for millions of American women just to go to a compounding pharmacy and get the exact right amount.

## WHY DOESN'T THE FDA APPROVE T FOR WOMEN?

It's a good question. There certainly is a need, as you might be acutely aware of. As usual, the amount of research on TRT for women is woefully lacking in proportion to the need for it. There's no controversy about testosterone's effectiveness; tests routinely prove that TRT dramatically increases libido, boosting sexual thoughts, fantasies, activity, and that ever-important satisfaction. That's why Australian, Canadian, English and other European women with hysterectomies or who are menopausal are happily filling their government-approved prescriptions for testosterone creams, patches and pellets every day.

One of the products available to them, but not to American women, is the bioidentical *Intrinsa* patch, by Proctor & Gamble Pharmaceuticals. It was tested for six months on women who had their ovaries removed and who also used estrogen. The results were stunning: satisfying sex increased 19% in the placebo group and 73% in the Intrinsa users. Frequency also increased.

Pleased with the outcome, P&G tried to get Intrinsa approved for women with hysterectomies, but the FDA voted it down in 2004 because of safety concerns. Remember, this was the year that the Women's Health Initiative results were revealed. With estrogen/progestin replacement getting a bad name, they were afraid to add testosterone to the mix. Plus they didn't want postmenopausal women to use it because it was untested on them.

---

**NOTE**» *OUR POSTMENOPAUSAL CANADIAN SISTERS HAVE BEEN GETTING GOVERNMENT-APPROVED T TO HELP THEM WITH THEIR SEX DRIVE SINCE 2002.*

---

Since 2004, big pharmaceutical companies have tried to get a product on the market but to no avail. *Estratest,* a combination of a pregnant horse urine derivative + synthetic testosterone *(methyl testosterone—or MET),* was available for a time. But their manufacturer, Solvay Pharmaceuticals, discontinued making it in 2009 because, although it had proved to the FDA it was safe, they hadn't proved to them that it was the T rather than the estrogen that made it effective.

## PROVING T MAKES A DIFFERENCE

Meanwhile, Proctor and Gamble Pharmaceuticals published the results of a yearlong double-blind trial in 2008 proving that bioidentical T does indeed work. They isolated its effects by using 814 women who had surgical or natural menopause and didn't use estrogen or E+progesterone. Patch in place, one group got 300 ug of testosterone a day, the

319

second 150 ug, and the third received the placebo. Both doses of T significantly upped desire compared to the placebo, but the women getting the 300 ug had more sex and the most fun: their libidos, arousal, orgasm, and pleasure were way higher than the women with the fake patches.

---

**NOTE»** *85% OF THE WOMEN WHO REPORTED THESE BENEFITS WANTED TO CONTINUE USING THE PATCH.*

---

Yay! It works. But is it safe?

## TESTOSTERONE REPLACEMENT THERAPY AND HEART HEALTH

Some physicians and researchers worry that replacing testosterone could increase the chance of getting heart disease since men have more heart disease than women. The majority of studies don't support that theory. After a review of the current information, doctors in the Department of Medicine at Cedars-Sinai in Los Angeles found zero adverse cardiovascular effects. Even more compelling, researchers of a six-month double-blind trial of 36 postmenopausal women with chronic heart failure found that those using the testosterone patch had more strength in their muscles and a greater ability to function in life. As a result they wound up recommending testosterone supplementation as "an effective and safe therapy."

Which do you think is better for a healthy heart? High T or Low T? Neither. Researchers who followed 639 postmenopausal women for 12 years determined that both increased cardiovascular risk.

## IS TRT SAFE FOR THE BREAST?

Some medical professionals are afraid that the T might convert to estrogen, raising the E high enough to cause breast and uterine cancer. What does current research show?

Let's look at the synthetics first. In another review of the Women's Health Initiative, researchers found a very small, statistically insignificant rise in invasive breast cancer when women used Premarin (CEE)+methyl testosterone (MET). The Nurses' Health Study, on the other hand, reached a more worrisome conclusion when they combed through their own statistics: they found that women who used CEE+MET had a 2.5 times greater risk of breast cancer than women who didn't use any hormone replacement at all, and an even larger risk than women who only used CEE.

---

**NOTE**» THE CEE AND THE MET WERE TAKEN ORALLY.

---

When it comes to transdermals, it's generally thought that there isn't real proof that transdermal T contributes to breast cancer.

There is, however, one iffy result. In the P&G trial you just read about a few pages back, breast cancer was detected in three women who used the testosterone patch as opposed to none in the placebo group. The researchers couldn't conclude that the T did or did not cause it because the first cancer was detected after just four months, meaning maybe it was growing before; a second woman reported having a bloody nipple discharge before the test began, meaning she did have it. That left the last woman and it was hard to tell if she would have gotten it anyway. A fourth woman, with a family history of breast cancer that included her sister, developed breast cancer after the tests were over.

## CAN ADDING TESTOSTERONE TO HORMONE REPLACEMENT ACTUALLY BE SAFER?

A woman's natural testosterone protects her breast cells from too much estrogen. And, according to some test results, women adding T to their estrogen+progesterone replacement does the same thing.

One study in South Australia, led by C. Dimitrakakis, followed 508 postmenopausal women using hormone replacement+T replacement for 5.8 years. They found the breast cancer rates for these women to be:

- Lower than for women who never used any hormone replacement

- "Substantially less" for women receiving Prempro (CEE+medroxyprogesterone acetate) in the Women's Health Initiative study

- 42% less for woman receiving estrogen/progestin in the Million Women Study

I read their study summary, but alas, the type of T, dose and delivery wasn't mentioned.

## COULD TYPE OF T, DOSE AND MEANS OF DELIVERY MAKE A DIFFERENCE?

Yes. TRT is safe, according to a Maturitas review, *"Safety of Testosterone Use in Women,"* if they use:

- Bioidentical testosterone

- A transdermal patch or gel

- And, very importantly, the same amount they naturally would make (hence the need for blood tests)

As a matter of fact, they determined that it might aid in the prevention of heart disease, breast and endometrial cancer.

---

**NOTE***» ANOTHER PLUS FOR TRANSDERMAL T IS THAT IT DOESN'T GO THROUGH THE LIVER, SO IT DOESN'T AFFECT CHOLESTEROL LEVELS. TAKING ORAL T LOWERS "HEALTHY" CHOLESTEROL AND RAISES "BAD."*

---

## BEARDED LADIES AND OTHER DREADS

If your lover is using testosterone, are there scary, hairy side effects? Fear not. If she is using the right dose, the side effects go from none to mild. The most common problems are acne, oily skin and facial hair. Researchers found that women would usually prefer to pluck a few hairs or use targeted skin products than to have a bad sex life. Sometimes, a lady's voice can deepen a little. Rarely, the size of her clitoris can increase a little, which is not necessarily a bad thing. A sign that she's getting too much T is when any of these get out of hand or she gets male pattern hair loss, smaller breast size, or becomes angry and hostile. Give her the right dose, and these reverse.

## BETTER SEX AND OTHER HOPES

So that you know, it's not just the sex that can get better in women once their climate has changes. TRT might help postmenopausal women with osteoporosis. Some small studies found it increased bone density in the spine and hipbone, which are frequent and dangerous areas for bone loss. Another study showed TRT improved verbal and memory skills. For sure we know it reduces fat and increases body mass.

## TESTS

As you can see, all the tests on Testosterone Replacement Therapy were done on women who had hysterectomies or were postmenopausal. What about the women who are in the midst of climate change? And what about long term effects? Almost every paper we read, on TRT—and HRT and BHT for that matter—pleaded for more long-term, large clinical trials.

# DECISIONS

Now you know what we know and have become an amateur hormone replacement expert. As you can see from all the info, using HRT or BHRT is not a do-it-yourself project. Women need to find informed, experienced doctors who know the pros and cons of each product, offer BHRT as an option, and can help decide what's right for them. There are so many variables to consider, starting with should a particular woman even use hormone replacement? What are her symptoms? How severe are they? How soon will they go away? What do they do to her quality of life or relationship? Does she have a history of disease or high risk of any, such as breast cancer or stroke? Will it help protect her against osteoporosis? Do the benefits far outweigh the risks in her particular case? A "yes" answer poses all those other questions about HRT or BHRT, dose, means of delivery and how long she should use it.

It sounds very complicated, but once a solution is found and a woman is comfortable with her choice, life gets easier. If hormone replacement is right for her, it can make a huge difference in her health and well-being during climate change, which is good for everyone. Whatever she decides, she can now focus on the joys of "older, wiser" and the new freedom that brings.

We hope this information helps you on your journey.

Happy Landings.

# ACKNOWLEDGEMENTS

What a joy it is to express our gratitude to all the smart, generous people who have helped us with So THAT'S Why They Do That! Men Women And Their Hormones.

We're lucky to have these wonderful friends who also happen to be consummate professionals.  A big thank you to:

Media gurus Joel and Heidi Roberts for their workshop in which they and a female participant, whose name we don't know, helped us formulate our Top Gun Love brand.

Heidi Roberts, who slogged through a super-rough first attempt at a manual and advised us to use more fighter stories and flying analogies.

Elayne Taylor, hard-boiled noir mystery author and editor, who read and advised us on the first real draft of the T, E and OT chapters. She has also been fiercely encouraging and unstinting in sharing her valuable publishing and marketing information and contacts.

Thomas Page, author, screenwriter and technical writer, who not only read the manual but, uninvited, did a gratis, six-hour line edit of it. He was also our 24-hour help line for grammatical and other errors.

Gina Gladwell, screenwriter, business writer and editor who, likewise, read the manual and was on standby for any problems or questions.

Thorough, perceptive readers Trey Alsup, Deborah Brock, Rundy Duphiney, Samantha Feller and Kelly Ann Ford whose meticulous notes and feedback made the manual so much better.

Glenda S. Owens RPh, MHA, who verified that the Pregnancy Chapter was accurate and Nahal Hakim, Pharm D, who checked the Hormone Replacement Therapy in the Appendix for any errors regarding compounding pharmacy prescriptions.

Dr. Cynthia Watson, who vetted the Pregnancy, Andropause and Menopause chapters with her sharp, experienced eye to ensure we didn't embarrass ourselves and mislead you with incorrect information.

Pam Tarlow, Pharm.D., Integrative Pharmacist, who with unerring support read and corrected the Hormone Replacement Therapy in the Appendix three times before it was right.

After So THAT'S Why They Do That! was completed, we relied on these great people to get it in shape and ready for publication:

Line editors Jenny Jensen and Tina Lewis.

Book designer Marael Sorenson.

Aspen Kuhlman and Stephanie Kruger at SO&SO Co LLC.

The brilliant Lee Roesner, who designed our front and back covers, created our website www.topgunlove.com and made the whole process fun!

Robin Blakely, our book, PR and marketing coach. She created order out of chaos, connected us to Lee and SO&SO, wrote the back cover, solicited testimonials, and much more. We couldn't have done it without her. Really.

THANK YOU ONE AND ALL!

# INDEX

331

333

336

339

344

345

346

# About the Authors

*So THAT'S Why They Do That!* is written by happily married relationship experts Judith Claire and Frank Wiegers. Judith founded her thriving Los Angeles counseling and coaching practice in 1978. Frank, a former fighter pilot, launched his encore career as a sex and relationship teacher and coach. Together, the couple has created the Top Gun Love series to help singles and couples realize their dreams.

# CONTACT US

Thank you for reading *So THAT'S Why They Do That! Men, Women And Their Hormones*. We hope it has given you greater understanding and some tools to create a better, more fulfilling love, sex and relationship life.

We'd love to get your feedback and to continue the conversation. We invite you to:

- Join our site *www.topgunlove.com*

- "Like" Top Gun Love on *Facebook*

- Follow us on twitter *@topgunlove*

And one last Smooth Takeoffs and Happy Landings!

Made in the USA
Coppell, TX
04 December 2020